POLARITY MANAGEMENT

IDENTIFYING AND MANAGING UNSOLVABLE PROBLEMS

Barry Johnson, Ph.D.

Published by HRD Press, Inc.
    22 Amherst Road
    Amherst, Massachusetts 01002
    1-800-822-2801

First Printing, August, 1992

ISBN 0-87425-176-1

Production Services by Susan Kotzin

Cover Design by Old Mill Graphics

TO DANA,

THANK YOU

Table of Contents

Introduction xi

Chapter 1   Teamwork Is Not a Solution 1

Chapter 2   Breathing New Life Into Your Organization 19

Chapter 3   The Misunderstood Leader .27

Chapter 4   Being "Right" Is the Easy Step 41

Chapter 5   Crusading and Tradition-Bearing 53

Chapter 6   A Problem to Solve or a Polarity to Manage? 79

Chapter 7   How to Recognize a Well-Managed Polarity
             When You See One 97

Chapter 8   Two Departments in Conflict 117

Chapter 9   Action Steps 129

Resources 139

Supplements 145

Section A   An Owner and a Manager Struggling with
             Change 149
Section B   "Tough/Love" in the Workplace 165
Section C   How Participatory Management Gets Into
             Trouble 181
Section D   The Joys of Stress and Tranquility 199
Section E   Generic Polarities 207
Section F   Values: The Art and Science of Polarity
             Management 225
Section G   Capitalism and Socialism:
             Neither a "Solution," Neither a "Mistake" 247

Appendix   Polarities List 263

Acknowledgments

The director and staff of the Human Resource Development Center (HRDC) at the University of Toledo believed in the potential of Polarity Management and have been a constant source of encouragement and support. From finding a publisher and reviewing the literature to making solid recommendations for improvements, doing research on applications, and helping with last minute collating, they have been there for me. I feel especially grateful to Joseph Spencer, Director of the HRDC, Joseph Hurst, Neil Vander Veen, Joseph Moyer, Pat Fisher, and Carol Mitton.

I am also grateful to Leonard Hirsch, President of the Institute for Strategic Management, whose friendship, combined with his work on paradoxical change in both management and politics, provided insight and reassurance.

Others have helped by reading various drafts and giving recommendations for improvements: Fay Kandarian convened a reading and feedback group of managers and professors in New Haven, Connecticut. Joseph Hurst convened another reading group at the University of Toledo. Other readers with helpful suggestions include: Marian Campbell, Richard Clarke, Don DeGuerre, Krishna Dighe, Kristin Dighe, Shalom Johnson, Jim Linton, John Otterbacher, Sallie Snyder, Jennifer Sumner, Bill Whitaker, and Dana Wilcox.

Jack Gibb, President of Omicron Associates, did not work directly on this book. Yet I gratefully acknowledge his influence on my life and my thinking. Jack, a mentor and friend, has always looked to the opposite of conventional wisdom for the truth contained in seeing the whole picture. This orientation is basic to Polarity Management. Jack also believed in me and encouraged me to write a book years before I believed enough in myself to do it.

Finally, I am extremely grateful to Don Benoit and Mary George, the primary editors, for their invaluable help in converting a rough text into a readable book.

About the Author

In the quest to understand organizations, Barry Johnson founded four of them: a 24-hour crisis intervention center, a community-based newspaper, a residential treatment center for addicted adults, and a manufacturing company. In the process, he received his Ph.D. in Organization Development from International College in Los Angeles.

For the past 15 years, Dr. Johnson has been an independent consultant in the combined areas of management development and organization development. He has worked in both the private and public sector in the United States, Canada, and Mexico. Clients have included General Motors, Michigan State Police, Southern New England Telecommunications, Syncrude of Canada, the Provincial Government of Ontario, Grupo Alfa in Mexico, FabriSteel Inc., and Westlane Industries.

Dr. Johnson has been working on the Polarity Management Model and set of principles since 1975. This book is in response to encouragement by many clients and workshop participants to "Get it in print."

Introduction

I have some bad news and some good news. The bad news is that there are a large number of unsolvable problems in your life, both at work and at home. I'm not talking about difficulties you could solve if you had more money, time, or other resources. I'm talking about difficulties that are inherently unsolvable, ones you cannot solve with resources.

The good news is that you can stop trying to solve them. Instead, you can improve your skills in identifying unsolvable problems and learn to manage them well. That is what this book is all about.

Current Trends are Polarities to Manage

Many of the current trends in business and industry are polarities to manage, not problems to solve. These trends are often described as movements *from* one way of thinking or acting *to* another. For example, it is currently popular to move:

- from neglect of the customer to focusing on the customer
- from individual to team
- from competition to collaboration
- from centralization to decentralization
- from a lack of quality consciousness to high quality consciousness
- from rigid structures to flexible arrangements
- from autocratic management to participatory management

These trends are making a contribution to increased effectiveness and are important for organizational survival. Seeing these movements as "problems to solve" radically undermines our ability to implement them. We define the problem as what we are going "from" and the solution as what we are going "to." For example, "We need to move *from the problem* of centralization *to the solution,* which is decentralization."

I suggest that each of these trends is better understood as a polarity to manage. As such, the principles of Polarity Management can be very helpful. Our problem-solving skills and the whole problem-solving paradigm, while extremely useful with solvable problems, can get in the way when we have a polarity to manage.

A different paradigm, Polarity Management, is a helpful complement to your problem-solving skills. You have been managing polarities all your life, some with more success than others. This book will enhance your ability to manage polarities, for those situations which call for it, by offering a model and a set of principles as an alternative to problem solving.

Polarities to manage are sets of opposites which can't function well independently. Because the two sides of a polarity are interdependent, you cannot choose one as a "solution" and neglect the other. The objective of Polarity Management is to get the best of both opposites while avoiding the limits of each.

For example, we constantly send managers off to "charm school" because they are too rigid (problem) and we want them to be more flexible (solution). The reason why managers often resist such training is that there is something they value about what is being called "rigid." They value clarity. Furthermore, there is something they are afraid of in this push toward "flexibility." They are afraid of "ambiguity." Those who resist know that flexibility alone is not a solution. A leader needs to be clear *and* flexible. This is a polarity to manage, not a problem to solve. The issues become, "How do you bring adequate clarity to a situation without being rigid?" and "How do you bring adequate flexibility to the same situation without being ambiguous?"

This only becomes relevant after letting go of the problem-solving paradigm where the problem is *a rigid manager* and the solution is *to get the manager to become more flexible.* Polarity Management involves seeing a more complete picture of the situation and respecting the wisdom of those who are resisting our "solutions."

All effective leaders "manage" the clear/flexible polarity. The polarity is unavoidable and unsolvable. With this polarity and all the others we face, the issue is not *if we are going to manage them,* but *How well?* This book will teach you "how."

Polarity Management Will Make You a More Effective Leader

Polarity Management skills will make you a more effective leader and manager by:

1) Increasing your ability to distinguish between problems you can solve and those you cannot.
2) Increasing your ability to manage those unsolvable problems which I call workplace dilemmas or polarities.

You will be more effective because:

1) You will save time and energy by not trying to solve those difficulties which are unsolvable.
2) You will have a better understanding of resistance to organizational changes you want to make.
3) You will be more effective in negotiating with those opposing your changes.
4) And you will be more effective in negotiating with those who are proposing changes you do not want.
5) You will be more effective as a third party mediator. This is especially true in conflicts where two groups are stuck in a polarity and they are treating the polarity as if it is a problem to solve.
6) You will be able to anticipate and minimize problems that occur when workplace dilemmas, or polarities, are not managed well.

7) Your decision making will improve. This is especially true with decisions where you must choose "both" sides of a set of apparent opposites.

Enough of list making. Chapter One leads us right into an important polarity for all leaders: Individual and Team. I will use that polarity as a focus for exploring some initial principles of Polarity Management.

CHAPTER ONE
Teamwork Is
Not a Solution

1

For every complex problem there is a simple solution.
And it's wrong.

— Anonymous

A Workshop Which Included Team Building

I conducted a workshop recently in which the key issue was team building. I was talking about Polarity Management and pointing out that TEAM was one pole of the INDIVIDUAL/TEAM polarity. One of the managers interrupted me. "Wait a minute," he said. "We have had this big push for team for over a year now. Are you saying that after all this effort and money, we will have to change everything and go in the opposite direction!?"

He was clearly upset at the prospect that the investment in team-work was somehow going to be discounted. His reaction was understandable. I told him that if his organization was emphasizing team and neglecting the individual, it could anticipate that some people would resist and that the organization would start to experience the downside of the team focus.

Immediately, others from the same company started giving examples of resistance to the push toward team. They also had examples of how the company was experiencing some of the downsides of the team focus.

Part of the reason the manager was upset was that he saw the team emphasis as a solution to an organizational problem. If I was questioning the solution then I must be calling team building a mistake. But the team emphasis was neither a solution nor a mistake. It probably *was* a needed focus for that organization at that point in time.

The managers in front of me wore a variety of expressions. Some were frowning and seemed a bit skeptical. Others had knowing smiles and seemed eager to see just how Polarity Management could

3

help them handle the team/individual dilemma. They would soon find out.

Polarity Management

I will introduce you to Polarity Management in an analysis of this Team/Individual issue. The dilemma was "How to support the IN-DIVIDUAL *and* support the TEAM." I asked the managers to help me fill out a Polarity Map by identifying the *upside* and *downside* of each pole, the "Team" pole and the "Individual" pole. Below is the Polarity Map, our starting point.

Figure 1:
Building the Individual/Team Polarity Map

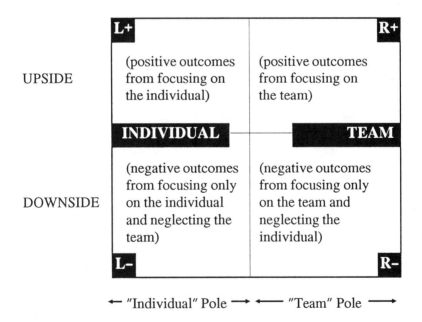

	L+	R+
UPSIDE	(positive outcomes from focusing on the individual)	(positive outcomes from focusing on the team)
	INDIVIDUAL	**TEAM**
DOWNSIDE	(negative outcomes from focusing only on the individual and neglecting the team)	(negative outcomes from focusing only on the team and neglecting the individual)
	L−	R−

← "Individual" Pole → ← "Team" Pole →

The Polarity Map is represented by two poles. The left half represents one pole, which in this case is the Individual. The right half represents the other pole, which in this case is the Team.

Each pole, INDIVIDUAL and TEAM, is also divided in half. The upper half of each pole represents the positive outcomes that result from focusing on that pole. These are the benefits of that pole or its "upside(s)." The plus sign (+) in the upper half of each pole is a symbol that means whatever is put in that quadrant is considered positive or good. (For consistency throughout the book, I will refer to the upper left quadrant as (L+) and the upper right quadrant as (R+).)

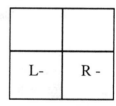

The lower half of each pole represents the negative outcomes that result from focusing only on that pole and neglecting the opposite pole. These are the disadvantages of that pole or its "downside(s)." The minus sign (-) in the lower half of each pole is a symbol that means whatever is put in that area is considered negative or bad. (I will refer to the lower left quadrant as (L-) and the lower right quadrant as (R-).)

In order to manage a polarity effectively, you will have to see all four quadrants of the Polarity Map. Seeing all four quadrants is "seeing the whole picture."

Back at the Workshop

Back at the workshop of managers, I displayed the drawing of the Polarity Map on a flip chart. With the four quadrants empty, we set about to create the whole picture by filling in each of the quadrants. I asked them what they wanted to accomplish with their recent emphasis on team. What I was looking for, primarily, was the upside of the team emphasis (R+).

There is no "correct" order for filling out the quadrants. When you do it, I suggest that you fill out whichever ones are easiest and expand from there. I chose the upside of team because I thought that would be the easiest quadrant for the managers to fill out. The completely capitalized words below are the ones that went on the flip chart. Here is what the managers had to say:

- "We had a problem with everyone trying to 'do their own thing.' And the company encouraged it. We ONLY REWARDED 'HOME RUNS.' We got ISOLATED from each other."

- Another manager chimed in, "We knew we needed to come together as a COHESIVE UNIT with a COMMON DIRECTION."

- "We want to create a sense that we are all in this together and EVERY PERSON'S JOB IS IMPORTANT."

- "We were also after that SYNERGISTIC EFFECT. You know, when a group of people get together and their individual ideas trigger ideas for others. They stimulate each other and generate more creative options than they would if they were each working alone."

- "There is also TEAM SUPPORT. When one person makes a mistake or needs help, others are there to help shoulder the load or pick up the pieces."

- "PERSONAL SACRIFICE," said another manager. "That's another thing we need. There are times when personal sacrifice is necessary to help the team accomplish its goal. We were getting too much SELFISH, 'ME' TALK among the troops and not enough 'we' talk. We weren't able to compete with those organizations where people were willing to put team needs ahead of personal needs."

As the information rolled in, it was clear that there were many good reasons to promote teamwork. The list indicated not only what benefits they wanted to get by team building (the upsides of team) but what they wanted to leave behind (the downsides of individual). At this point, we had some solid content for two of the four quadrants on the flip chart. Figure 2 shows a cleaned-up version of our results.

Figure 2:
Individual/Team Polarity (Partial Map)

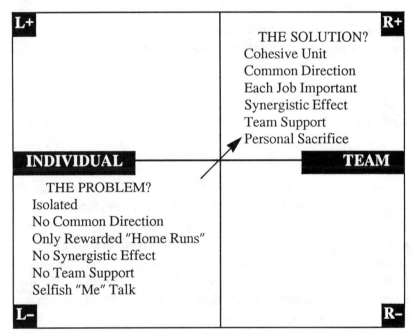

Whenever there is a push for a shift from one pole of a polarity to the other, it is because those pushing are:

1) Experiencing or anticipating the downsides of the present pole which they identify as the "problem," and,

2) They are attracted to the upsides of the other pole which they identify as the "solution."

In other words, whoever was encouraging the outlay of time and money for this organization's team building was moving *toward* something and moving away from something else. In terms of the Polarity Map in Figure 2, it is easy to see why, if an organization was experiencing the downside of over-focusing on the individual (L-), they would consider it a "problem" and want to move away from it. At the same time, it is easy to see how the upside of team (R+) would be seen as a "solution," and why they would want to move toward it.

Though the move from the downside of the individual (L-) toward the upside of team (R+) is probably a good move, even a necessary one, it is not a solution. The reason it is not a solution in any final sense is because you cannot just focus on team to the neglect of the individual. Such a singular, permanent focus will result in less effective teams and less effective individuals because:

If you focus on the team to the neglect of the individual, you get the downside of team.

Let us return to the discussion with the managers and see how that works. It was clear from looking at the flip chart (Figure 2, above) that we were working with only half the picture. In order to manage this polarity effectively, we need to fill out the other two quadrants: the downside of team (R-) and the upside of individual (L+). To identify the downside of team, I asked them what difficulties they were experiencing with their new team emphasis. Again, they were not at a loss for words:

- One manager, who seemed particularly upset with all the "yea team" talk, jumped in right away. "I'll tell you what I'm hearing. People don't like the feeling that they have to think and act like everyone else in order to be a 'team player.' We are getting TOO MUCH CONFORMITY. Next thing you know, we'll all have to dress alike. It is really undercutting INDIVIDUAL INITIATIVE and CREATIVITY."

- "I agree," said another. "We are creating a long list of do's and don'ts to make sure everyone gets treated the same. Who wants BLAND SAMENESS?"

- A third manager continued the list. "We are having TOO MANY MEETINGS and they LAST TOO LONG. And it's not just the number of meetings. You also feel like you can't do anything until you clear it with the team. I agree with Bob, we are stifling those individuals who really are creative and eager to step out and do something."

- "Whatever happened to the ENTREPRENEURIAL SPIRIT we talked about a few years ago?" asked another manager. "What we are doing now is settling for the LEAST COM-MON DENOMINATOR in order to include everyone on everything. There may be such a thing as team support but there is also the possibility of TEAM BURDEN and we seem to be experiencing it."

- Another manager, who had been silently watching the process unfold, added some of his reflections: "You know, the thing that Ben said earlier about personal sacrifice was a good point. But that cuts both ways. If you push the personal sacrifice thing too far, people end up NEGLECTING PER-SONAL NEEDS for the sake of the team or the organiza-tion. This is leading to some real resentment and some problems at home."

Notice that this input not only identifies the downside of team (R-), it also identifies aspects which are the upside of individual (L+). It is similar to what happened when we were identifying the up-side of team (R+) and received a number of comments on the downside of individual (L-). This happens because *the clearest op-posites in the Polarity Map are the downside of one pole and the upside of the other.* (L-) and (R+) are such strong opposites that you

	R +
L -	

can make a list in either quadrant, put "not" in front of it, and you will have the beginnings of a list for the other, diagonal quadrant.

The same is true for the other pair of diagonal quadrants: (L+) and (R-).

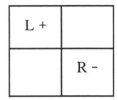

We now had information listed in all four quadrants giving us a working description of the whole picture. Polarity mapping gave structure to the dilemma. It looked something like this:

Figure 3:
Individual/Team Polarity (Completed Map)

L+	R+
Individual Initiative	Cohesive Unit
Individual Creativity	Common Direction
Entrepreneurial Spirit	Each Job Important
Meetings: Fewer-Shorter	Synergistic Effect
Individual Freedom	Team Support
Addressing Personal Needs	Personal Sacrifice
INDIVIDUAL	**TEAM**
Isolated	Too Much Conformity
No Common Direction	Bland Sameness
Only Rewarded	Meetings: Too Many—
"Home Runs"	Too Long
No Synergistic Effect	Least Common Denominator
No Team Support	Team Burden
Selfish "Me" Talk	Neglect of Personal Needs
L–	R–

Now that we can see the whole picture (the STRUCTURE of the dilemma), we can begin to see how it works (the DYNAMICS of the dilemma). *The normal movement through the four quadrants can be pictured as an infinity loop (∞). I call it the "Polarity Two-Step."*

Polarity "Two-Step"

The Polarity Two-Step starts in either lower quadrant and moves as follows:

> 1) Across and Up
> 2) Down

> *now repeat*

> 1) Across and Up
> 2) Down

Presto! You have gone through all four quadrants and are back where you started. Let's look at Figure 4 (below) to see how it works. Figure 4 is a simplified version of our Figure 3 Individual/Team Polarity Map.

Figure 4:
Polarity Dynamics

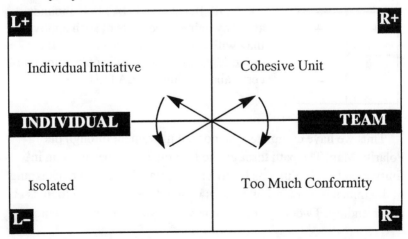

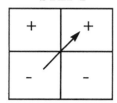

STEP 1

ACROSS and UP

When an organization experiences too much ISOLATION of individuals or individual departments, there will be a tendency to move (Step 1) "Across and Up" in an effort to become a more COHESIVE UNIT.

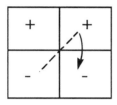

STEP 2

DOWN

As they become a more COHESIVE UNIT and gain the benefits of such a move, they will eventually experience the move (Step 2) "Down" as people voice concerns about TOO MUCH CONFORMITY.

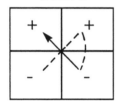

STEP 1

ACROSS and UP

When an organization experiences TOO MUCH CONFORMITY of individuals or individual departments, there will be a tendency to move (Step 1) "Across and Up" in an effort to encourage more INDIVIDUAL INITIATIVE.

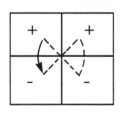

STEP 2

DOWN

As INDIVIDUAL INITIATIVE abounds and they gain the benefits of such a move, they will also eventually experience the move (Step 2) "Down" as people voice concerns about being ISOLATED.

Thus we have completed the normal movement through the Polarity Map. The path through the four quadrants becomes an infinity loop (∞). I think this is most appropriate because the managing of dilemmas is an ongoing process which, like the infinity loop, is never-ending. Twenty years from now, if I were to have a reunion with the managers from the workshop and they were still working, they would still be managing the Individual/Team dilemma.

Then, like now, *the question would not be "If" they are going to manage the polarity, but "How well?"*

At first glance, this may seem both simple and academic. But think for a minute about the millions of dollars that are spent each year promoting "team building." Now think of all the time and money that is invested to promote "individual initiative." When either of these efforts are treated like a problem to solve rather than as part of a polarity to manage, the effort is much less effective than it could be. In Polarity Management terms, you will:

1) Generate unnecessary and costly resistance, and

2) Spend needless time in the downside of one or both of the two poles.

On the other hand, Polarity Management perspective and skills can make you more effective by increasing your ability to:

1) Anticipate and work with resistance, and

2) Get the "best of both worlds" by keeping your team primarily in the upsides of the Individual/Team polarity.

The potential benefits both in quality of work life and in cost savings are considerable just in this one polarity. But the real potential is in your increased ability to manage a variety of polarities both in your work life and in your non-work life. The chapters ahead will cover some of those polarities and give you the tools for identifying and managing others.

Summary

1) There is a distinction worth making between a problem you can solve and a dilemma (polarity) you will need to manage.

2) If you have a dilemma to manage, the Polarity Map provides a STRUCTURE for addressing the whole picture. The structure is a square divided into four parts. The right and left halves are called poles. The upper part of each pole contains the positive aspects of that pole or its "upside(s)." The lower part of each pole contains the negative aspects of that pole or its "downside(s)." Creating and discovering the content of all four quadrants is essential for maximum effectiveness in managing a dilemma.

3) Once you have a working picture (map), you can begin to anticipate outcomes because there is a predictable, normal movement through the map. This "normal movement" is part of the DYNAMICS of Polarity Management. The push for movement in a polarity is for a shift to the other pole. This push comes from those who are: A) anticipating or experiencing the downsides of a pole from which they want to *move away* and, B) attracted to the upsides of the opposite pole which they want to *move toward*. The downside pole they want to leave often becomes identified as the "problem." The upside of the opposite pole becomes identified as the "solution."

This push creates the movement from the downside of one pole to the upside of the other pole, either "A" or "B" below, which is Step 1 in the Polarity Two-Step, ACROSS AND UP:

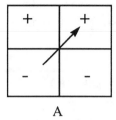

A

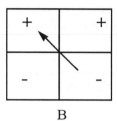

B

With time, a focus on one upper quadrant as a "solution," and the relative lack of attention to the original pole, the movement continues to the downside of that pole, either "A" or "B" below, which is Step 2, DOWN:

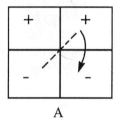

A

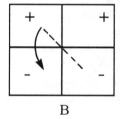

B

THEN REPEAT = Step 1 and 2 are repeated as the system moves through all four quadrants, making the pattern of an infinity loop:

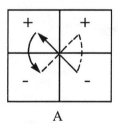

A

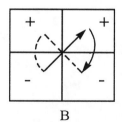

B

Exercise

1) You may want to try your hand at describing a polarity that you would like to manage better. Think of some ongoing difficulties at work where you feel like you have to make a choice between opposites. Begin by listing the two poles.

_____ AND _____
       (Left Pole)   (Right Pole)

Here is a list of some common polarities. You may choose to use one of these for this exercise.

Cost	and	Quality
Market Driven	and	Product Driven
Centralized	and	Decentralized
Innovation	and	Standardization
Autocratic	and	Participatory
Process Engineering	and	Product Engineering
Planning	and	Taking Action
Common Computer Systems	and	Custom Computer Systems

2) Now identify some upsides and downsides to each pole.

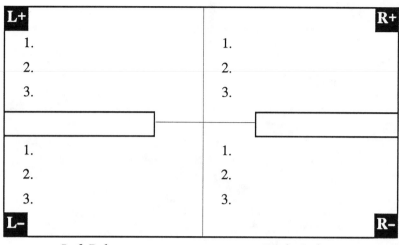

Left Pole	Right Pole

3) Does the "Normal Movement" through the model correspond to your experience with this polarity? Do you feel like moving away from the downside of the situation you are in and toward the upside of the opposite? Knowing the content of all four quadrants and understanding the normal flow is a good start to managing this polarity.

CHAPTER TWO
Breathing New Life
Into Your Organization

2

Whatever goes around, comes around.

— Anonymous

Breathing Is a Polarity Management Process

I would like you to try a guided experience. Inhale slowly and deeply for 10 seconds, *then hold it!* If breathing is a problem to be solved by choosing to *either* inhale *or* exhale, I have just provided you with a solution by telling you to inhale. Though inhaling is essential and feels good at first, you soon find yourself sinking into the downside of inhaling, filling up with too much carbon dioxide.

Now exhale slowly during the next 10 seconds, *then hold it!* Notice the relief as you clean out the carbon dioxide. Though exhaling is essential, you soon find yourself sinking into the downside of exhaling with a need for fresh oxygen. Now inhale again and breath naturally.

Figure 5:
The Breathing Polarity

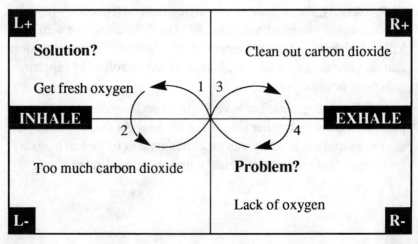

L+		R+
Solution?		Clean out carbon dioxide
Get fresh oxygen	1 3	
INHALE	2 4	**EXHALE**
Too much carbon dioxide		**Problem?**
		Lack of oxygen
L-		R-

You do not solve the exhale/inhale polarity by choosing to *either* inhale *or* exhale. You manage it by getting the benefits of each while appreciating the limits of each. It is not a static situation. It is a process, an ongoing flow of shifting emphasis from one to the other and back again. Managing this polarity requires choosing BOTH inhaling AND exhaling.

The Breathing Organization

Imagine, if you will, a meeting of the top twenty people in a two thousand employee company. They are trying to agree on the company's direction for the next five years. One key element is to decide whether they are going to be an inhaling or an exhaling organization.

After heavy negotiations and some clever politicking, they decide that inhaling is definitely the wave of the future. A vocal exhale minority says it is a big mistake, but reluctantly join a unified effort at inhaling.

As people start turning blue, the exhale minority says, "We told you so!" A shake-up at the top follows and an exhaler is put in charge to rescue the operation. Inhaling was clearly a mistake, and so the obvious solution becomes "exhaling." Thus determined, "exhaling" is pronounced as "the new direction for the decade."

Predictably, the organization will be in as much trouble with this solution as they were with the old one. The difficulty is not with inhaling or exhaling. Both are essential. *The difficulty is the perception that they are dealing with a problem that can be solved by choosing* either *one* or *the other.*

This breathing metaphor is very simple and obvious. Many workplace dilemmas are neither simple nor obvious. At the same time, its simplicity and obviousness can be a strength. Let us look at it again for insights that might help us deal with more complicated issues.

Just as it is foolish to see inhaling and exhaling as a problem to be solved, it is foolish to treat personal, organizational and international polarities as if they can be solved and not managed.

If you follow your breathing process through the model in Figure 5, you will notice that the there is a natural movement through the four quadrants in the pattern of an infinity loop. Understanding this normal flow can help us manage it better. You understand that you do not have to worry about shifting from inhaling to exhaling for fear that you will never come back to inhaling. You know that it will not be long before the shift to the exhaling pole will reach the limits of its benefit and you will return to inhaling. It would be a disaster to believe that you needed to stay at the inhaling pole because if you shifted to exhaling you would never return to inhaling. In such a situation, *the fear of getting stuck in the opposite pole gets you stuck in your own pole. The more you stay stuck in your pole, the more you experience the downside of your pole.*

When a "solution" does not work, it will be called a mistake, as in the breathing metaphor where the organization decided on inhaling. Inhaling was seen as a "solution" until it did not work, then it became a "mistake." But it was neither a solution nor a mistake. It was half of a polarity that needed managing through an ongoing shift in emphasis between inhaling and exhaling.

There is a paradoxical relationship between the poles. Though inhaling and exhaling are opposites, they are part of the same whole. One cannot exist without the other. *In order to gain and maintain the benefits of one pole, you must also pursue the benefits of the other.* The ability to inhale the greatest amount of fresh air requires that first you exhale as completely as possible. These opposites are, paradoxically, interdependent. This is true of the many polarities we encounter every day.

In terms of the breathing metaphor, part of what a leader is hired to do is to help the organization "breathe." You can "breathe new life into your organization" by helping it flow more easily back and forth between the poles of key polarities as they need attention. You can help your organization get unstuck when it seems to be holding its breath out of some fear of moving from the present pole to the opposite one. This is no small contribution.

Summary

1) "Either/Or" thinking must be *supplemented* with "Both/And" thinking in order to effectively manage dilemmas.

2) There is a paradoxical relationship between the two poles. They are interdependent opposites.

3) Seeing the upside of one pole as a "solution" is a set-up for it to be called a "mistake" later on.

Exercise

Coaching Through Critical Analysis and Encouragement

Think of a person or project team that is reporting to you and has a project started but not finished. One key polarity that you manage as you receive their progress reports is providing CRITICAL ANALYSIS on the one hand, and ENCOURAGEMENT on the other. What, in your mind would be the benefits (upside) of your providing them with CRITICAL ANALYSIS of their reports? Write your answer in the upper left quadrant (L+). What would be the negative consequences (downside) of giving only CRITICAL ANALYSIS and not giving any supportive ENCOURAGEMENT? Write that answer in the lower left quadrant (L-).

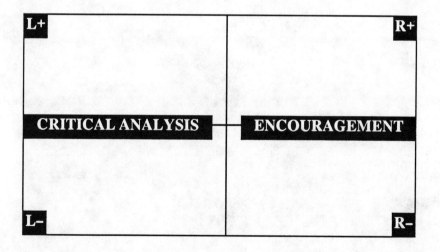

What would be the benefits (R+) of providing them with EN-COURAGEMENT for continuation of their effort? Write that answer in the upper right quadrant (R+). What would be the negative effects of giving only ENCOURAGEMENT and neglecting CRITI-CAL ANALYSIS? Write that answer in the lower right quadrant (R-).

People tend to give much more weight to the *critical analyses* they receive than to their *encouragement*. Thus, we need to give more encouragement than critical analysis if we want people to feel the encouragement as strongly as the critical analysis.

When you look at how you have responded to your employees' progress reports so far, would you say that they are getting solid amounts of both critical analysis and encouragement? Are you over-emphasizing one pole or the other? If you are over-emphasizing one pole, you are probably getting more of the downsides of that pole than you would like. What could you do to manage this polarity better when your employees come to you with their next report? Give it a try.

CHAPTER THREE
The Misunderstood Leader

3

One way to change people is to see them differently.

— Barry Stevens

Should a Leader Be Clear or Flexible? Yes.

It is more effective to be clear *and* flexible than to focus on one or the other. If you just focus on being clear, you will be seen as rigid. If you just focus on being flexible, you will be seen as ambiguous or "wishy-washy."

This rather simple truth came out of hundreds of interviews with workers and leaders from several organizations. These interviews were done in situations where there were serious problems between workers and their bosses. I was called in to listen to all parties and make recommendations for improving the situation.

There were two types of criticisms of leaders which kept showing up in my interviews:

1) He or she is too RIGID. The boss was described as stubborn. "He won't listen." "It's my way or the highway!"

2) The second set of complaints identified a different problem. He or she is too AMBIGUOUS. The boss was seen as too "wishy-washy." "You never know where she stands."

For each of these sets of criticisms, there was an automatic solution proposed by the workers.

1) The RIGID boss should become more FLEXIBLE. He should listen to reason. She should be willing to adjust to new circumstances.

2) The WISHY-WASHY boss should be more CLEAR. She should let us know what she is expecting. He should have a clear direction and stick with it.

It is difficult to disagree with the solutions these workers propose if you buy their descriptions of their bosses. So why not just tell RIGID bosses to be more FLEXIBLE and tell AMBIGUOUS bosses to be more CLEAR?

We do! And it seldom produces the results we desire. One reason these obvious solutions do not work is that we are dealing with a polarity which needs to be managed but treating it as if it were a problem to solve.

Take a look at this situation from the perspective of the boss. Those leaders who are accused of being RIGID by their employees often felt good about how CLEAR they were. They would say things like: "At least they know where I stand. If I say, 'one more absence this month and you're gone,' they know I mean it." Or, "This place needs some clear structure and accountability. Without it, you just have chaos."

Those leaders who are accused of being WISHY-WASHY by their employees often felt good about their FLEXIBILITY. They would say things like: "I think it is important to listen to the employees and make adjustments on the run." Or, "Everything is changing so fast, those who are stuck RIGIDLY in the old ways are just not going to make it. FLEXIBILITY is the key these days."

Seeing the Whole Picture

The leaders and the employees have important and accurate perspectives on this dilemma. Workers who define the "problem" as their boss being too rigid have a ready-made "solution." He or she should become more flexible.

Their picture might look like the one on the next page.

Figure 6:
Employee View

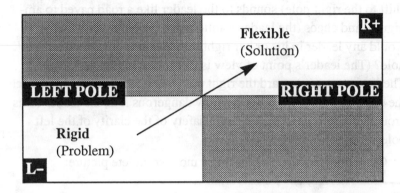

When their view of the boss is like Figure 6, both the problem and the solution are perfectly obvious. So obvious, in fact, one could easily get frustrated with a boss who could not see it. How could someone possibly be opposed to the very logical move from the left pole to the right pole, from being rigid to being flexible? Such a person, the workers would argue, has no business being a boss.

Figure 7:
The Leader View

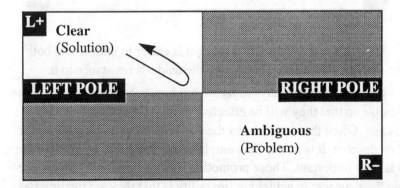

31

The very same behavior the workers call being rigid (a problem) the leader calls being clear (a solution to an anticipated problem)! Not only that, the solution proposed by the workers (that the leader shift to the right pole) sounds to the leader like a road paved to ambiguity and chaos (the leader's anticipated problem). Now why would any leader in his or her right mind want to jump into such a hole? (The leader's point of view is illustrated in Figure 7 above.) The leader moves toward the right pole much as one would approach the edge of a cliff. Then, seeing how dangerous it is, the leader turns around and returns to the apparent safety of the clarity of the left pole.)

Combining both views, we get a more complete picture:

Figure 8:
Combined Views

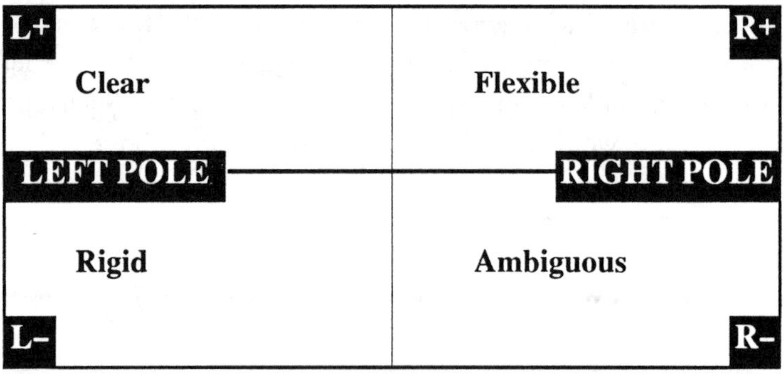

L+		R+
Clear	Flexible	
LEFT POLE		**RIGHT POLE**
Rigid	Ambiguous	
L–		R–

With this more complete picture, it is easier to understand both the worker's desire for change and the leader's resistance to it.

It is popular these days to figure out how to make managers more flexible so that they will be effective in the midst of accelerating change. Often those who resist these efforts are not given the credit they deserve. It is not that the emphasis on flexibility is unimportant. It is very important. Those promoting it have a point. What is reducing their success in achieving flexibility is that they are treating flexibility as a solution to a management problem. Flexibility is not a solution to a problem. Neither, of course, is clarity. Both are important aspects of an ongoing dilemma. Those who see either as a solution are seeing only part of the picture and will have difficulty understanding why they are getting resistance to their perfectly logical solution.

Using the same model, let us take a brief look at the opposite type of complaint that came out in the interviews. Just as some leaders overemphasize clarity and are accused of being rigid, other leaders overemphasize flexibility and are accused of being ambiguous. Those workers who criticize their boss for lacking decisiveness or direction have their solution in hand—"Be more clear about what you want and where you stand. Provide some leadership. Give some direction."

Their view of the situation might look like Figure 7 above. From this perspective, it is obvious what is wrong and how to correct it. The boss should move from the lower right quadrant to the upper left. It is a problem to be solved with a self-evident solution. Why would an intelligent boss resist such a move?

Having seen the whole picture of the model, it is quickly obvious from where the resistance will come. The leader might view the situation like Figure 6 above.

In judging the workers' criticism, the leader senses some naiveté about how complicated and dynamic the management process is. The workers do not seem to appreciate the need for flexibility. Their request for clarity sounds like a simplistic demand for rigid structures and directions that the leader knows will not stand the test of time. What the leader sees as his or her strength is being criticized and rejected in favor of something that seems loaded with bad consequences.

As with the push for flexibility, the push for clarity is more likely to lead to effective management if it is seen as a part of an ongoing process of managing an important polarity, rather than as a problem with an obvious solution.

The Misunderstood Leader

Let me tell you a true story.

I was involved in a retreat with a Vice President of a major U.S. business and his executive staff. I will call him "Sam." As I was presenting on Polarity Management and the clear/flexible dilemma, Sam lit up with a knowing look on his face and said, "I just figured out what has been going on in our division."

Sam had been brought in several months earlier to take over the division. There had been considerable turnover in recent years in this V.P. position. When Sam arrived, he decided that what the division needed was a clear vision and direction. They also needed some clear guidelines as to what he meant by this vision and direction.

His sense was that there was too much uncertainty and ambiguity, and his contribution would be to provide direction and get everyone moving with a common vision and in a concerted way. His view of the situation looked like this:

Figure 9:
Sam's View of Division's Problem and His Solution

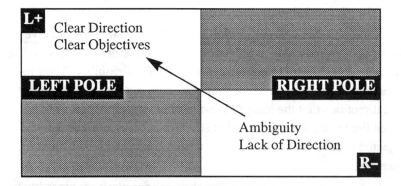

He saw the uncertainty, ambiguity, and lack of direction as a problem to be solved and the obvious solution was to bring clarity to the situation. Sam's efforts to improve the division were based on an assessment of what it needed at that time. He saw the division as located in the lower right quadrant and needing to move to the upper left. The arrow indicates the drive to move in that direction.

Sam worked long and hard with his executive staff to carve out the direction and guidelines for the future. He held division-wide meetings and many subdivision meetings to make sure the message was understood.

The greater his effort at clarity, the more frustrated he became. For example, Sam had a goal of faster project turnaround time in order to be more responsive to the market. To be more clear in moving toward this goal, he said he wanted all projects to be completed within two years rather than the traditional six-year average.

People started asking questions and raising issues over his proclamations. In the name of clarity, he repeated himself and became even more specific. What was happening in Polarity Management terms was that his valiant efforts to be clear were being interpreted by his subordinates as signs of rigidity. The more complete picture looked like Figure 10 (below).

Figure 10:
Clear/Flexible Polarity Map

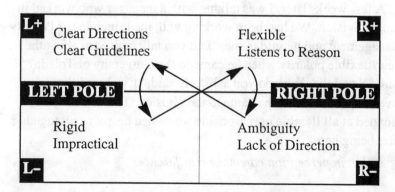

Sam's efforts at clarity were experienced as being rigid and impractical. As he met with questions and resistance, he thought the problem continued to be lack of clarity so he would repeat himself in new, creative, and more precise ways. This only *increased* the perception that he was rigid and impractical! The objective of those with questions and resistance was to gain from Sam some flexibility in his guidelines. They wanted him to "listen to reason." Sam's subordinates wanted him to move to the upper right hand quadrant.

As Sam saw the whole picture of the Polarity Model and understood the dynamics of how it works, he started to laugh at himself and the situation. He said to me, "Do you suppose that when I told people that I wanted all projects completed in two years, they thought I meant twenty-four months?!" I said, "Sam, you are dealing with a bunch of engineers. They probably thought you meant 104 weeks." Sam laughed again at the thought of himself being seen as rigid. He said,"All I meant was that we need to move toward two years and away from six years. I was trying to give clear direction and a target to shoot at."

He then asked how to correct the situation. We talked about how he could be clear *and* flexible in his communication to the division. He could say to them just what he had said to us in the meeting—that he wanted to move in the direction of faster project completion cycles and that about two years was a target. He could also "listen to reason" and indicate some flexibility in his expectations when people identified significant problems with the time lines that were set.

A few weeks later, I was talking with a manager who worked in Sam's division. We had been working with the principles of Polarity Management and he said to me, "Did you talk with Sam about the clear/flexible polarity when he came to the University of Toledo?" I said, "Yes, I did. Why do you ask?" He said, "I've heard Sam give several speeches since he came to the division. The first time he sounded at all flexible or reasonable was when he got us all together after being here."

A shift in perception can make a difference.

Summary

1) Behavior which can be criticized from one perspective (seeing its downside) often can be praised from another perspective (seeing its upside).

2) The benefits of "flexibility in leadership" is important, and so is the "clarity-of-message" that some leaders fear could be lost in the process.

3) Seeing a "rigid" leader as "valuing clarity and wanting to avoid ambiguity" can help you work more effectively with him or her.

4) Seeing a "wishy-washy" leader as a person "valuing flexibility and wanting to avoid rigidity" can help you work more effectively with him or her.

5) In this chapter, I did not have a name for each pole at the ends of the line which separates the upsides from the downsides. Sometimes that is not necessary in order to understand and manage the polarity. In this case, I just used the essential characteristics of the two upper quadrants (clear and flexible) as a way to name it.

Exercise

What's My Preference

It might be helpful in understanding Polarity Management if you thought about it in terms of your own preferred way of doing things as a leader. For example, when you think about the clear and flexible polarity, which pole do you prefer, and therefore, tend to emphasize?

L+ Clear They know where I stand	Flexible I listen to reason R+
LEFT POLE	**RIGHT POLE**
Rigid My way or the L- highway	Ambiguous Wishy-washy R-

Obviously both are important and I believe that all of us use both flexibility and clarity in our work. At the same time, I think most of us have at least a slight preference for one over the other. I tend to favor the right pole. I do so either because I have a high value on flexibility or because I want to avoid being seen as a rigid "dictator." Or both. In my case both fit.

What this suggests in terms of my managing this particular polarity is that I tend to err on the side of flexibility. People I work with, especially those who have a strong preference for clarity, at times consider me too ambiguous.

I use their input to help me manage the polarity better. If I am too ambiguous for my colleagues, I recognize that I have probably emphasized flexibility a bit too much and shift from the lower right quadrant to the upper left with a concerted effort to be more clear.

If you are one of those people who tend to prefer clarity, you will tend to err on the side of the left pole. Those emphasizing this side do so either because they place high value on clarity or because they want to avoid being seen as an ambiguous "wimp."

Or both.

If your preference is clarity, people you work with, especially those who have a strong preference for flexibility, could, at times, consider you too rigid. You can use their input to help manage this dilemma. If you are being too rigid for your colleagues, you can recognize that you probably have emphasized clarity too much and can shift from the lower left quadrant to the upper right quadrant in a concerted effort to be more flexible.

The point is not that you should change your preference or that you should emphasize both poles equally. Instead, I am suggesting that seeing the whole picture can help you manage the polarity better. You know you can shift emphasis to the other pole any time you want and that you can always shift the emphasis back again.

Can you think of a situation where you overemphasized your preferred pole and experienced some of the downsides of that pole?

If so, welcome to the club. It happens to all of us as we do our best to manage this dilemma.

Can you think of a situation where you made a real effort to try out your less preferred pole? Sometimes this can feel very awkward, and it is easy to fall on your face. When that happens, you end up even more leery of that less preferred pole. I encourage you to hang in there and at least keep that less preferred pole available as a resource. Having access to both poles of a polarity is necessary in order to manage it effectively.

CHAPTER FOUR

Being "Right" Is the Easy Step

4

Accuracy and Completeness

I am using the terms "accuracy" and "completeness" in a fairly narrow and confined way to get at some important aspects of Polarity Management.

The Gestalt concepts of FIGURE and GROUND are helpful in understanding my meaning:

The picture on the left is a classic. Is it a goblet or two heads facing each other? The answer is, "It depends on how you look at it."

The picture is constructed so the goblet stands out for most people at first glance. It is the "figure" you see while the two heads are "ground" or in the background.

Figure 11: Goblet or Two Heads

If you are having trouble seeing the two heads, rotate the page until the goblet is straight up and down.

The instant you see the two heads, they have become your "figure," and the goblet has become background or "ground." Once both the goblet and the two heads are apparent to you, it is easy to shift quickly back and forth between the two.

This picture can help make the distinction between accuracy and completeness. If someone says, "This is a picture of a goblet," he is accurate. If another person says, "It's two heads," she also is accurate. What is figure for one is ground for the other. Both are accurate. But neither is completely correct; neither is describing the entire whole.

It is the incompleteness combined with the conviction of the rightness (accuracy) of their perception which is the source of a potential problem. The man and woman just mentioned could argue for days as to whether the picture is a goblet or two heads. They are both "right," but that is the easy part. Clearly seeing the alternative picture sometimes is the hard part. When you do not see the alternative picture but someone else claims it exists, it is honest and helpful to say, "I don't see it." It is naive and foolish to say, "It is not there." The difference between these statements is no trifle. The first provides a basis for help from the one who sees the alternate picture. The second will generate amazing resistance from the one who sees the alternate picture because you are contradicting their reality.

For example, if the man tells the woman, "You are wrong. There are no heads in this picture," he has gone beyond asserting the accuracy of his view. He is challenging the accuracy of her view. He is contradicting her reality. He has now set himself up for some serious resistance. She knows the heads are there. She sees them!

Likewise, if the woman tells the man, "You are wrong. There is no goblet in this picture," she is in for trouble. He knows what he sees with his own eyes. He will not accept statements that contradict what he knows to be true.

In order to end the argument, each must move from figure to ground. Neither should be asked to contradict or deny their view. Instead, each person's view is confirmed as "accurate." Then each is asked to *supplement* their view with a second view which is also true.

She does not have to give up her claim that there are two heads in the picture. She needs to let the heads move from figure to ground and let what is background in her perception (the goblet) become figure. In doing so she will be able to see the picture more completely.

She will be more open to looking for the goblet *after* her view of the two heads has been confirmed as accurate. When someone says, "Yes, you're right. I see the two heads," her reality is confirmed and she can more easily open up to expand or supplement that reality. She can let go of what was figural and let something from the background become the new figure. In this case, she can let go of the two heads for a moment and look for the goblet.

He has to do the opposite to see the picture completely. He has to let go of the goblet as the only reality in order to see the two heads. Again, he can more easily look for the heads *after* someone confirms the accuracy of his perception of the goblet.

But who goes first? What if she just cannot see the goblet and he just cannot see the heads? At this point, one or both of the parties might realize, "Hey, maybe this is not a situation in which we have *either* a goblet *or* two heads. Maybe this is a situation in which we should be looking for *both* a goblet *and* two heads in the same picture. We could both be accurate."

Now the whole challenge shifts. *Instead of contradicting each other's view, the task is to supplement each other's view in order to see the whole picture.* Each of them has key pieces to the puzzle. *Paradoxically, opposition becomes resource.* The statement becomes, "I don't see it. You say it's there. Help me see it."

The accuracy of each person is no longer being challenged. On the contrary, it is being assumed. This allows for a joint effort in combining two perfectly valid (accurate) views in order to see a more complete picture.

This example, like the breathing metaphor, is quite simple. It is easily seen that we have *both* a goblet *and* two heads. Because it is so obvious, it makes the *either/or* argument look silly.

Yet, *in our organizations, there are often very serious and costly confrontations that take place because a "both/and" polarity is treated like an "either/or" problem to solve.*

In the two pictures below, notice the parallel between seeing the goblet in Figure 12 and seeing the two diagonal quadrants (RIGID) and (FLEXIBLE) in Figure 13. In both cases, what is light is figural (prominent) and what is black is background. You need to see the two heads within the black to see the whole picture in Figure 12.

Similarly, you need to see what is within the black in Figure 13 in order to see the whole polarity.

 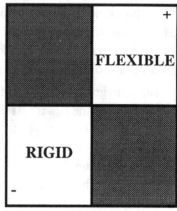

Figure 12: Goblet?   **Figure 13: Rigid to Flexible?**

To assume there is nothing in the black area in either picture is to mistake accuracy for completeness. Thus, being "right" is the easy part. Finding the "rightness" within the opposite point of view is the challenge.

For example, let us say that you have a supervisor working for you who is having some trouble with a number of the people in his area. The workers see him as "rigid" and think he should be more "flexible." They are seeing the white, diagonal quadrants (L-) and (R+) in Figure 13. It is similar to their seeing the goblet in Figure 12. They are "right." To tell them their supervisor is not rigid and does not need to be more flexible is to deny their reality. It is like saying the goblet does not exist. Such a contradiction of their reality will seriously undercut your ability to work with them. It also undercuts the possibility of this polarity being managed well.

46

If you do not see their boss as "rigid," you can say, "I don't see it. You say he is 'rigid.' Help me understand how you see him that way." When you have come to understand what the workers mean by "rigid" and how they see it applying to their supervisor, you can say, "I see what you mean." This is like saying, "Okay, I see the goblet."

But the workers are still at the easy step, being "right" (accurate). Now comes the harder step, which is being complete. Granting the accuracy of their perception that their supervisor is sometimes "rigid" and needs to be more "flexible" is not enough. There is more to the picture than meets their eyes. Since seeing the whole picture is fundamental to managing the polarity well, they need to supplement their view.

In terms of the picture analogy (Figure 12), they need to see the two heads. In terms of the polarity in Figure 13, they need to see what is in the two black quadrants (L+) and (R-). They may not be willing to take the harder step and look seriously for some content in the two black quadrants. You have increased the possibility that they will look by:

1) *Not contradicting their reality.* You did not say, "Your super-visor isn't rigid. I think he is plenty flexible." That would have been as naive and foolish as looking at Figure 12 and saying, "There is no goblet."

2) *Confirming their reality.* You took the hard step to see the situation from their point of view. You saw how the super-visor could be seen as "rigid" at times and how at those times some "flexibility" could help.

You have done what you could to "Walk a mile in their shoes." Now it is time to suggest to them that there is more to the picture.

You might say something like, "Look, you've made some valid points about Jim and we will address them. As we do, I think it would be helpful to appreciate his perspective. Jim likes to have order and structure in his area. He likes to be clear about where he stands on issues. That isn't all bad. What drives him up the wall is the feeling that things are falling between the cracks. We need to figure out a way to keep some of the structure and clarity we need, without it getting too rigid for you who work with him."

Certainly this situation is oversimplified. Yet, I think you can see how knowing the difference between accuracy and completeness can be a helpful tool. Furthermore, seeing the whole picture would help you be more effective with the workers, with Jim, and with any discussion that you might promote between them.

Letting Go to Get More

Look at Figure 12 again. Notice that both the goblet and the two heads cannot be perceived at the same time. Either one stands out and is clear or the other one stands out and is clear. Though you can shuttle back and forth quickly, to see the goblet sharply requires that you "let go" of the two heads.

Try one more example. Look out a window and get a clear picture of something in the distance. Now shift your focus to the glass in the window itself. Now shift back and forth between the object outside the window and the glass in the window. In order to see one clearly, you need to let go of the other. "Letting go" of the glass in the window does not mean you believe it is no longer there or that you cannot return to it. But letting go does mean that it is no longer the center of your attention. What you gain by letting go of the glass as the only figure is the opportunity to gain even more. You have the opportunity to see clearly what is beyond the window.

Self-Empowerment and Control

This brings me to the issue of self-empowerment and control. *It is easier to expand your view than to get those with an opposing view to expand theirs.*

Exploring an oppositional view requires a willingness to temporarily let go of your own view and put some effort into seeing and understanding the other's view. You are in control of the decision to let go of *your* view and to put *your* effort into seeing the other's view. You are not in control of the decision on the part of other people to let go of *their* view and put forth *their* effort at seeing your view.

In the example with the supervisor and the workers, you could not control whether they would let go of their image of Jim as someone who is simply rigid and needs to be more flexible. Nor could you control their willingness to look at possible upsides to his rigidity or downsides to the flexibility they wanted. What you could control was your own willingness to let go of your perspective and to invest in theirs. The least you get out of it is a chance to see a more complete picture that will increase your effectiveness in managing it.

In conclusion, there are at least four reasons for looking beyond your own view:

1) Because someone else sees it differently.
2) In order to expand your own reality.
3) If you can see another's point of view, he or she is more likely to accept an invitation to see yours.
4) If you have a polarity to manage, seeing the other half of the polarity will help you manage the situation better.

One final point before leaving figure/ground. In the picture, without the goblet (light space) there would be no heads. Also, without the heads (dark space) there would be no goblet. Neither part can exist without the other. Again we have the paradoxical relationship of interdependent opposites.

Summary

1) There is a difference between ACCURACY and COMPLETE-NESS.

2) Contradicting someone's accuracy generates unnecessary resistance.

3) Confirming someone's accuracy increases the possibility they will supplement it with yours.

4) To see the accuracy of the other person's view requires a temporary letting go of the primacy of your own view.

5) It is easier to expand your view than to get your opposition to expand theirs.

6) Once you have seen the accuracy of the other person's view, it becomes relatively easy to shift back and forth between the two perceptions.

Exercise

Is the picture below of an older woman or of a younger woman?

If you don't see both, find someone who sees the one you don't see and ask them to help you see it.

If you do see both, show the picture to a group of friends and see if you can find one who sees only the older woman and another who sees only the younger woman. Have them show each other the accuracy of their view until they both see both.

Notice how easy it is to see the first pic-

ture and how clear it is to the one who sees it. The ease of seeing it that way can make it difficult to understand how anyone could not see it. This ease and clarity can also get in the way of seeing the alternative picture.

Notice, also, how there is a need to let go of the primacy of one view (it being figural) in order to let the more hidden view (background) become the new figure. Once you have seen both pictures, it becomes relatively easy to move back and forth between them, with one being temporarily figural while the other is background, and then the reverse.

CHAPTER FIVE
Crusading and
Tradition-Bearing

5

The test of a first-rate intelligence is the ability
to hold two opposed ideas in mind at the same time and
still retain the ability to function.

— F. Scott Fitzgerald

Crusading and Tradition-Bearing Forces at Odds in the "Individual/Team" Dilemma

This chapter is about the dynamic tension in all polarities over *whether* to shift to the opposite pole, *when,* and *how.* Within that tension there are two major forces at work: crusading and tradition-bearing. I will explore the dynamics of this struggle but will first begin by clarifying the setting, which is the Polarity Map of the Individual/Team dilemma.

In Chapter One I filled in the four quadrants of the individual/team dilemma as closely as possible with words generated by the group of managers at the workshop. What I will do here is identify for each quadrant a somewhat more universal set of items that will make this polarity more applicable to a variety of situations. The revised polarity is shown on the next page.

I will move through each of the four quadrants following the normal flow (infinity loop) and summarize what I mean by each of the items. The words from the model will be in CAPITAL LETTERS.

The upside of focusing on the INDIVIDUAL (L+).

I think each of us wants to experience his or her UNIQUENESS, the fact that we are one of a kind. There is a certain amount of FREEDOM which is necessary to experience that UNIQUENESS. It is in this quadrant that we encourage INDIVIDUALS TO DREAM and to take on challenging personal GOALS. Personal FREEDOM and vision are part of what drives INDIVIDUAL INITIATIVE and CREATIVITY. We sometimes call it the "entrepreneurial spirit." There is also value in the ability to take CARE OF YOURSELF

55

which we often praise as "self reliance" or "rugged individualism."
All these things make an extremely powerful argument for focusing
on the INDIVIDUAL.

Figure 14:
Individual and Team

L+	R+
Uniqueness Freedom Ind. Dreams and Goals Ind. Creativity Care of Self	Connectedness (Belonging) Equality Common Direction and Goals Team Support Care for the Team
INDIVIDUAL	**TEAM**
Isolation Loss of Equality Loss of Common Dir. and Goals Loss of Team Support Loss of Team Synergy Selfishness	Sameness Excessive Conformity Loss Ind. Dreams and Goals Loss of Ind. Initiative Loss of Ind. Creativity Neglecting Self
L-	R-

The downside of focusing on the INDIVIDUAL (L-).

At the same time, if we focus on just the individual and neglect
the team, we get some very negative results. If you focus only on
your uniqueness and do not pay attention to being a part of a team,
uniqueness becomes ISOLATION. Freedom will always benefit
some more than others. If we pursue our freedom and neglect the
need for some degree of equality, the gap between the "haves" and
the "have nots" will grow into an extreme LOSS OF EQUALITY

with increased ISOLATION and resentment. Every individual pursuing his or her "dream" without attention to a COMMON DIRECTION AND GOALS will end up with a dissipation of energy and confusion, which benefits neither the individual nor the team. An over-focus on individual creativity can result in the LOSS OF TEAM SYNERGY, and individual initiative can be overplayed with a resulting LOSS OF TEAM SUPPORT. And, finally, care for self without attention to the needs of the team becomes SELFISHNESS. This disturbing list of downsides can make the shift to the upside of team seem very attractive.

The upside of focusing on the TEAM (R+).

Just as we want to experience our uniqueness, we also want to experience our CONNECTEDNESS. We want to know that we BELONG. Our EQUALITY as human beings is highlighted in this quadrant along with the conviction that we deserve EQUAL treatment. We recognize that everyone's job is important to the TEAM'S GOAL. We look beyond our personal dreams for ourselves and join other team members with a COMMON DIRECTION and shared GOALS. The sense of CONNECTEDNESS increases as we all "put our shoulders to the wheel" and give clear focus to our collective energy. TEAM SYNERGY gets tapped as team members stimulate and augment each other's contribution. The TEAM becomes more powerful than individuals acting alone as we take pride, together, in our TEAM accomplishments. TEAM SUPPORT gets us through hard times as those in trouble are backed up by their teammates. Individuals demonstrate "team spirit" by their willingness to make personal sacrifices in order to CARE FOR THE TEAM and accomplish its GOALS. In the military, many have given their lives for their team and the larger mission. All of these things make an extremely powerful argument for focusing on the team.

The downside of focusing on the TEAM (R-).

At the same time, if we just focus on the team and neglect the individual, another set of negative results occur. When we overemphasize our connectedness and the "one big happy family," we can neglect our need for uniqueness. "Belonging" degenerates into a bland SAMENESS. The emphasis on equality without adequate regard for freedom results in EXCESSIVE CONFORMITY. Attention *only* to team direction and goals results in a LOSS OF INDIVIDUAL DREAMS and GOALS. The emphasis on team support gets overplayed with a corresponding LOSS OF INDIVIDUAL INITIATIVE. Pursuit of team synergy also can be overdone. The result is both an underestimation and an undermining of INDIVIDUAL CREATIVITY. And, finally, the notion of personal sacrifice in order to care for the team, without attention to individuals taking care of themselves, leads to a loss of self reliance and NEGLECT OF SELF. This second disturbing list of downsides can make the shift to the upside of the individual seem very attractive. With this summary of the more general characteristics of the Individual/Team Dilemma in mind, let us look at the two major forces at play within it.

The Crusading Force

Those CRUSADING are the ones who want to move from the downside of the pole, where the group has been located, to the upside of the opposite pole, which has not been emphasized recently. In United States business and industry, the emphasis in recent years has been toward team and increasing teamwork. In terms of the concept of Figure/Ground, what is figural (most prominent) for those in an organization promoting teamwork are the two quadrants with clear content in Figure 15, on the opposite page.

When these two quadrants are figural, it is easy to understand why they would be promoting the move away from the individual focus and toward team. *The greater the difference in clarity about the content of the two sets of diagonal quadrants, the stronger someone will feel about the "rightness" of their position and the "wrongness" of their opposition.* For example, if those crusading for team are *very clear* about the downside of individual and the upside of team (one set of diagonal quadrants), and *very unclear* about the upside of individual and the downside of team (the other set of diagonal quadrants), they will feel *very right* about their crusade and think that

Figure 15:
Crusading with a "Team" Focus

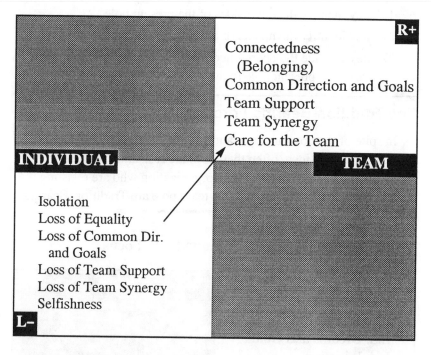

those opposing them are *very wrong*.

From this perspective, it is easy to see how crusaders, blind to the upside of what they are complaining about and blind to the downside of the "ideal" situation toward which they are crusading, can become self-*RIGHT*eous and extremely frustrated with those who oppose their crusade.

At the same time, crusaders are essential to the health of the system. They are the push to inhale when the organization has been exhaling too long or the urge to exhale when the organization has been inhaling too long. To ignore them or stifle their crusade leads to a poorly managed polarity which is foolish in the short run and costly in the long run.

Those CRUSADING are the change agents. They see some problems with the present and want to make things better for the future. They make three contributions to the managing of this dilemma:

1) They identify the downsides of the present pole.

2) They identify the upside of the opposite pole.

3) They provide the energy necessary to move from the downside of the present pole to the upside of the opposite pole.

The Tradition-Bearing Force

In spite of the obvious logic and general agreement that team-building is a good idea, often there is some resistance to the effort, either overt or covert. Those in the organization who are resisting the shift from the individual pole to the team pole are Tradition-Bearing.

Figure 16:
Tradition-Bearing with an "Individual" Focus

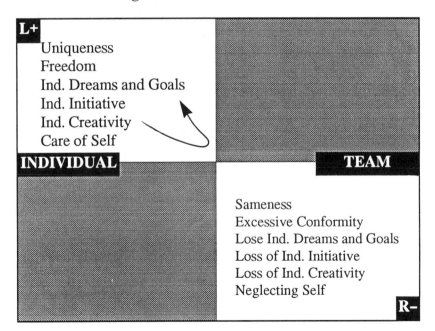

They are the preservers of what is best from the past and the present. For them, what is figural (prominent) is the set of diagonal quadrants opposite from what is figural for those crusading.

TRADITION-BEARERS for the "Individual" focus place a high value on the upper left quadrant and have considerable fear of falling into the lower right. From the perspective in Figure 16, it is easy to see why they would resist the move from individual to team. From their perspective, team has no upside and a host of downsides.

Here again, the greater the difference in clarity about the content of the two sets of diagonal quadrants, the stronger those tradition-bearing will feel about the rightness of their position and the wrongness of those crusading. If those who are tradition-bearing are blind to the downside of the present pole and the upside of the pole toward which the crusade is headed, they can be equally self-*RIGHTe*ous and frustrated with those promoting this crusade.

At the same time, tradition-bearers are essential to the health of the system. They are the ones who encourage the organization to breathe deeply and get the most out of each breath. To ignore them or stifle their tradition-bearing leads to a poorly managed polarity which is, again, foolish in the short run and costly in the long run.

Those TRADITION-BEARING make three contributions to the managing of this dilemma:

1) They identify the upside of the present pole, which are things that should be maintained or preserved.
2) They identify the downside of the opposite pole, which are potential problems they want to avoid.
3) They provide the energy necessary to preserve the upside of the present pole and to avoid the downside of the opposite pole.

With the contributions of those who are *crusading* and those who are *tradition-bearing,* we have the contents of all four quadrants. We also have some oppositional energy to work with. Managing this oppositional energy is part of the art of working effectively with dilemmas.

One step in managing the polarity is to get out of the "EITHER/OR" mind-set, i.e. "We have to decide whether we are going have a bunch of prima donnas running around here OR whether we are going to work as a team." Notice how this quote reflects only two of the four quadrants, which results in a clear problem and an obvious solution. It is a quote from an "either/or" mind-set. Put in the Polarity Map, it would look like this:

Figure 17:
Team-Oriented, "Either/Or" Mind Set

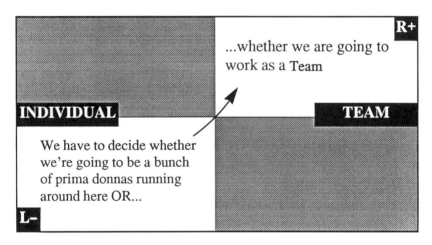

Both those *crusading* and those *tradition-bearing* may have this "either/or" mind set. When they do, the whole issue boils down to one of power.

When the CRUSADING FORCES get into an "either/or" power battle with the TRADITION-BEARING FORCES, no matter who wins, they both lose. They both lose because *the result of an either individual or team fight will be to end up primarily in one of the lower quadrants.*

If those tradition-bearing "win" and the work group ignores the concerns of those crusading for Team, the group will end up in the downside of Individual. The process will look like arrow number 1 in Figure 18:

Figure 18:
Ineffective Tradition-Bearing (1) and
Ineffective Crusading (2)

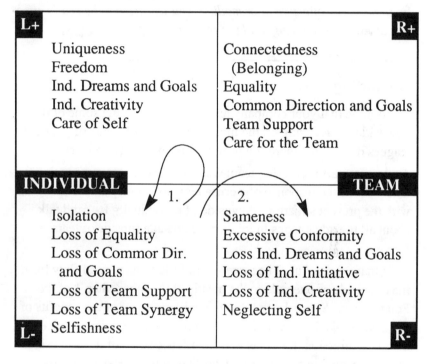

If those crusading "win" and the work group ignores the concerns of those tradition-bearing to protect the Individual, the group will end up in the downside of Team. The process will look like arrow Number 2 in Figure 18. In either case, the group or organization will not benefit from the results.

As a leader, you can improve your effectiveness considerably if you are able to lead effective crusades and lead effective tradition-bearing efforts. I know that right now all the hype centers around being a great leader of change, and that orientation seems to support the crusading forces. But what I am suggesting is that effective change management requires the ability to be both a crusader and a tradition-bearer. It also means dealing well with your opposition and with the "undecided" who are not sure which way to go. Paradoxically, *to be really effective at crusading, you will need to be really effective at tradition-bearing, and the reverse.*

Crusading

Assume that your company has been experiencing some of the downsides of focusing on the individual. You and some of your colleagues decide that there is a need to improve the team work.

As you start promoting team work you encounter some resistance. Often the response of a crusader is to identify all the problems with the present situation (downside of individual = L-) and talk about all the advantages in joining the crusade (upside of team = R+).

If that works, fine. The system will follow the normal flow from the downside of one pole to the upside of the other (Step 1 of the Polarity Two-Step = L- to R+). You will get some of the benefits of the upside, like feeling more "team spirit," and be relieved to have a common direction. Later, as you experience some of the downsides of team (Step 2 of the Polarity Two-Step = R+ to R-), hopefully you will recognize them and be willing to move back to the upside of individual (R- to L+).

Ineffective Crusading

But what if you cannot convince people to join your crusade? What if your clear, rational identification of the "problem" (the downside of individual) and your logical "solution" (the upside of team) does not result in your desired change in poles?

With accuracy and rightness on your side, you decide to restate your case more eloquently and powerfully than before. If the resistance persists in spite of your eloquence, you can always commiserate with others in your crusading group over the half truth that "Everyone resists change."

If rational argument does not work, crusaders often take the next step which is to try overpowering or getting around those who are tradition-bearing. Then you get into an "either/or" power struggle and, as I mentioned earlier, even when you win, you lose. The net result is that your crusade will be ineffective.

The goal of any crusade is not "victory" over the tradition-bearers. There is no such thing as victory over the tradition-bearers. That would be like saying, "The goal of inhaling is to 'defeat' exhaling." It will not happen, unless inhaling also comes to an end. *The goal of any crusade, from a polarity management perspective, is to maximize the upsides of each pole while minimizing the downsides.*

With that goal in mind, and some understanding of the principles of Polarity Management, let us look at another tack for you to take on your crusade for team.

Effective Crusading

As you start promoting team work you encounter some resistance. You know this is a dilemma to be managed and not a problem to be solved. From that perspective, you know this resistance could be a potential resource. Your strength is that you know the problems with the present situation (downside of individual) and have a clear vision of what would improve the situation (upside of team). You have a clear view of half the picture.

You also know that there probably is an upside to the things you have been complaining about and a downside to where you want to go. You know that in order to manage this polarity well, you need to know what is in all four quadrants.

Furthermore, you know that the basis of the resistance is in the tradition-bearers' perception of reality. They are afraid of losing whatever in their mind is the upside of individual (L+) *and* they are afraid of getting stuck in whatever in their mind is the downside of team (R-). In terms of Figure 19 (below), they have built a wall between their two fears.

Figure 19:
Effective Crusading—A Wall Becomes a Bridge

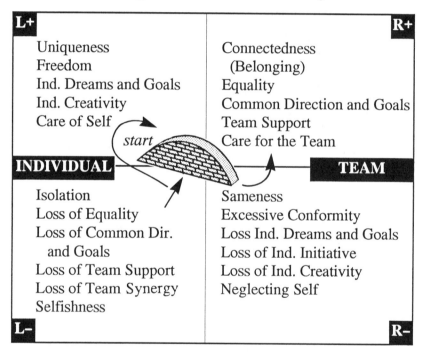

L+	R+
Uniqueness	Connectedness
Freedom	(Belonging)
Ind. Dreams and Goals	Equality
Ind. Creativity	Common Direction and Goals
Care of Self	Team Support
start	Care for the Team
INDIVIDUAL	**TEAM**
Isolation	Sameness
Loss of Equality	Excessive Conformity
Loss of Common Dir.	Loss Ind. Dreams and Goals
and Goals	Loss of Ind. Initiative
Loss of Team Support	Loss of Ind. Creativity
Loss of Team Synergy	Neglecting Self
Selfishness	
L-	R-

Because of this wall, you can not follow the normal movement of the Polarity Model. When the normal flow is blocked, turn around and go in the opposite direction. Rather than increase the pressure to break down the wall, make it a bridge. Include the wall in your process of getting to where you want to go.

In doing this, you are going through the four quadrants in the opposite direction from the normal flow: (L+) to (R-) to (R+). In this process of getting the polarity unstuck, you are taking the time to identify and incorporate the concerns of the tradition-bearers into the process. Without identifying those concerns, you would not have the whole picture, which means you would be limited in your ability to manage the polarity.

By going counter to the normal flow, you not only are joining the resisting forces by seeking their reality first, you also are joining, temporarily, the direction of their energy. They are wanting to slow down or stop the normal flow through the polarity because they are afraid of where it seems to be headed. By moving against the normal flow, you are "going with" their resistance.

This is a paradoxical orientation toward change. *The easiest way to get the benefits of team when encountering resistance is to identify the benefits of the individual and acknowledge the limits of team.*

Your job is to listen to the tradition-bearers. They will help you see the whole picture. As I mentioned before, people are more likely to hear you after they feel heard. If you can first confirm their reality, they are more likely to be open to expand that reality to include yours.

When you go to the upside of individual (L+), make sure you know what is there. If you do not know, ask. Those tradition-bearing will welcome a chance to help you see it!

When you are clear about what is there, let the tradition-bearers know that you are aware of this quadrant and that you, like them, want to preserve it. Say things like, "It is very important to me that we not lose sight of the individual in this process. We have some people who show great individual creativity and initiative and we need to figure out a way to keep that spirit alive."

Now the "wall" becomes a "bridge" as you go to the downside of team (R-) and make sure you know what is there. Again, you let the tradition-bearers know that you are aware of this downside and that you, like them, do not want to get bogged down in those problems. Say things like, "I sure do not want us to get into some 'group think' where everyone has to think alike and act alike. I know that too much group pressure for conformity can be a bad thing."

By going to the two quadrants that the tradition-bearers are concerned about, you have forced yourself to see the whole picture so you can manage it better. You have also let the tradition-bearers know that you are not a simplistic complainer who believes there is no upside to individual, nor a naive dreamer who sees no downside to where you want to go.

You have also disarmed the tradition-bearers by incorporating his or her reality rather than contradicting it. You have increased considerably the likelihood that the tradition-bearers, having been heard, will listen.

At this point, you go to (R+) and share your vision. Tap the dreamer in you. Describe what you think is possible, what you are excited about. The tradition-bearers know that this is not a completely naive vision because you have already acknowledged the upside of the present and the downside of where you want to go. You have walked the "bridge" rather than only beating on the "wall."

You might say something like, "Without ignoring some of the problems you have identified, I'm excited about the possibility of our having some creative and energetic teams here. We can blend our talent into a very competitive force."

Last, and only if necessary, you can go to the downside of individual (L-) and identify some of the problems you see. "Right now we have a collection of talented people, but we lack that special ingredient of pulling together as a team. We seem to be going in too many different directions."

Notice that you end up at the downside of team (L-) rather than start there. I think it makes a difference to conduct a crusade from this perspective. It will greatly improve the chances that this polarity is managed well.

Effective Tradition-Bearing

I have spent most of my life crusading. I worked as a community organizer, founded a few organizations, and felt very invested in making things "better." I guess I still do more crusading than tradition-bearing.

But after more than one disastrous crusade, I tried to gain some perspective on what the process was all about. I also started consulting with men and women who owned and ran companies. I found a new appreciation for them and the people who came before them. Some of these men and women spend much of their time tradition-bearing. I have learned a great deal from them about respecting what has been built by others and about preserving what is good from the past and present. Let me describe what I have learned from them about effective tradition-bearing.

Imagine that you are a leader in a company that is having some difficulties but that also has a solid history of getting through hard times. A few other leaders come to you with a series of complaints about how there needs to be more coordination of effort. "Everyone seems to be doing their own thing. The company only rewards 'home runs' by individuals. We need to start rewarding work groups as a group for their collective efforts." They also suggest changes such as doing away with personal parking spaces and getting company uniforms so that you can increase the sense of equality and comraderie. "And let's get everyone involved in the decisions so that we can get some commitment to those decisions." The list could continue.

As I mentioned before, tradition-bearers often see those crusading as naive complainers who do not appreciate how well off they really are. In terms of Figure 20 (below), tradition-bearers frequently respond by identifying the good things (upside of individual L+) about the present situation and the bad things (downside of team R-) that could happen if the crusaders got their way. Operating from this perspective, they figure out ways to resist the crusade. Again, it can get into an "either/or" fight in which the organization ultimately loses.

69

There is an alternative tack for tradition-bearers who see this as a dilemma to manage rather than a problem to solve. The process is essentially the same as the one mentioned for crusading. *Start by getting yourself clear about **their** perception of reality rather than starting by trying to convince them of yours.*

Figure 20:
Effective Tradition-Bearing

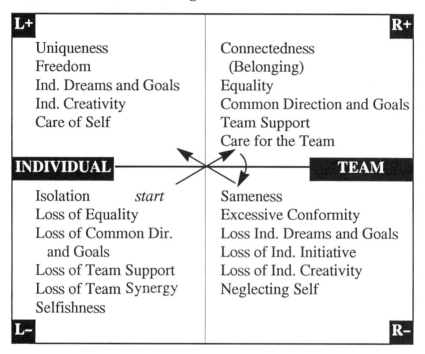

Instead of starting at the upside of individual (L+) and going to the downside of team (R-), start in (L-), go to (R+), then (R-) and finally (L+).

As one who is now aware of the dynamics of the polarity map, you know there is a need to shift focus back and forth in order to manage the dilemma. You also know that you need to see all four quadrants to manage the situation well. So you listen closely to what the crusaders are saying. Make sure you understand what they are concerned about (the downside of individual L-) and where they want to go (the upside of team R+).

Then you let them know you are aware of those two quadrants and, like those crusading, you consider them very important. After they know that you understand their concerns and desires, you can then let them know what you are afraid of (the downside of team R-) and what you value (the upside of individual L+). Notice that as a tradition-bearer, you not only joined the crusaders by trying to see their reality first, you also moved through the quadrants *with* the direction of movement they wanted to pursue. By making the trip through the quadrants in this fashion, you gain some credibility and get a more complete picture of all four quadrants. You also increase the possibility of being heard. It is worth the trip.

The objective of the effective tradition-bearer is not to block crusades but to join them and challenge them at the same time. To join them is to recognize that the situation is a polarity that needs managing. That means there will be regular times when there needs to be a shift in focus from individual to team, and that it will shift back again. To challenge them is to make sure the upside of individual does not get lost and the downside of team does not get ignored.

Again, the goal is the ongoing, effective management of this dilemma, which is to stay as much as possible in the upper two quadrants.

I have written about the Crusading force and the Tradition-Bearing force in terms of the individual/team dilemma. These two forces are at the heart of the struggle within all dilemmas. What excites me about Polarity Management is that it can help you be more effective in dealing with a particular dilemma, whether you are crusading, tradition-bearing, or being a third-party mediator.

Summary

1) There are two necessary oppositional forces at play in all dilemmas: *Crusading and Tradition-Bearing.*

Crusading—This force comes from the awareness of the downsides of the present pole (the one the organization is currently emphasizing), and the upsides of the opposite pole. Those crusading want to make things better. For them, this is done by shifting to the upside of the opposite pole.

Strengths:

— Will not ignore the downsides of the present pole. Listening to their concerns can help the system self-correct in a timely fashion.

— Show respect for what "could be." Provide vision and energy for moving to the other pole.

Limitations:

— Can be blind to the upside of the present pole and to the downside of the pole they are advocating.

— Seen as "complainers" who are unappreciative of the past and present.

— Seen as naive "dreamers" unaware of the downsides of the "promised land" toward which they are crusading.

— Generate unnecessary resistance by treating the situation as a problem to solve in which they have identified the problem as the downside of the present pole and the solution as the upside of the other pole.

Tradition-Bearing—This force comes from the awareness of the upsides of the present pole and the downsides of the opposite pole. Those tradition-bearing want to preserve what is good about the present and avoid things getting worse. For them, this can be done by staying in the upside of the present pole.

Strengths:

— Give legitimate warnings about shifting to the other pole. Listening to these warnings can reduce the likelihood of falling quickly and disastrously into the downside of the opposite pole.

— Show respect for "what is." Provide vision and energy for staying in the present pole.

Limitations:

— Can be blind to the downsides of the present pole they are preserving and to the upsides of the pole they are avoiding.

— Seen as resisting change, living in the past, and lacking vision.

— Generate unnecessary resistance by treating the situation as a problem to avoid, in which they have identified both the problem to avoid as the downside of the other pole and the solution as the upside of the present pole.

2) These two forces need each other to manage a polarity well. If either force overpowers the other and neglects the value of the other, you end up spending unnecessary time in the downside of the "winner's" preferred pole.

3) If a person or system is "stuck" in the downside of one pole, you need to reverse the normal flow to get "unstuck."

4) Effective Polarity Management means being good at tradition-bearing, good at crusading, and good at third party mediation between those crusading and those tradition-bearing.

5) The goal of Polarity Management is to maximize the upsides of each pole and minimize the downsides.

Exercise

Below is an exercise of filling out a polarity map (creating the whole picture) and then looking at guidelines for talking to your opposition.

1) Pick a dilemma you would like to explore. You may want to:

a) return to the one you created at the end of chapter one,

b) identify a new one that is a present concern in your organization, or,

c) use one from the list below.

Structured and Unstructured	Individual And Team
Centralized and Decentralized	Specific and General
Self Reliance and Other Reliance	Cost and Quality
Market Driven and Product Driven	Planning and Producing

2) Put the two words on either end of the neutral axis in positions L and R.

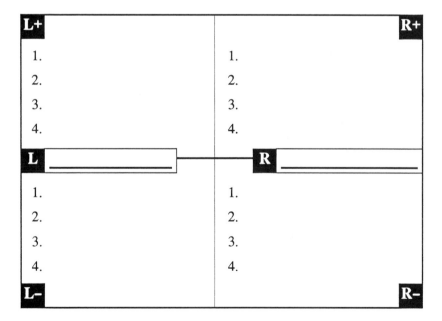

3) Now fill out the four quadrants: L+, L-, R+, and R-.

Here are some guidelines to help you think about what is in each quadrant:

— The L+ quadrant contains the many benefits that an organization gets by focusing on the L pole. Try to list three or four benefits.

— The L- quadrant contains the downsides you get when you focus only on L and neglect the R pole. Try to list three or four downsides.

— The R+ quadrant contains the many benefits that an organization gets by focusing on the R pole. Try to list three or four benefits.

— The R- quadrant contains the downsides you get when you focus only on R and neglect the L pole. Try to list three or four downsides.

If you are having trouble thinking of something for each of the four quadrants, I suggest you either pick another polarity for this exercise or ask an associate how he or she would fill out the troublesome quadrant(s).

4) If you have the Polarity Map filled out, we can create guidelines for effective communication between those crusading and those tradition-bearing in your polarity.

Let's say the ones crusading are a group who think the organization is in quadrant R- and they want to move to L+. They are getting some serious resistance from a tradition-bearing group who think the organization is in R+ and who are afraid this group of naive complainers are going to get the system into L-.

Effective Crusaders Communicate:

In this situation, those crusading are most likely to be heard by their opposition if they talk about the four quadrants in which order?

_____   _____   _____   _____ (answers follow)

Answer: With the assumption that those who feel heard are more open to hearing, I suggest those crusading talk first about R+, then L-, L+, and R-.

Though this is mechanical, I would like you to try the following lead-ins to the lists you have created in the four quadrants. As a crusader for a move from R- to L+ talking to your opposition, you might say something like:

- "I know you think (read R+ list) are all very important. I do too. And I do not want us to lose them."
- "And I certainly do not want us to get into (read L- list)."
- "Yet I would like us to figure out a way to get (read L+ list)."
- "Because I'm concerned about (read R- list)."

Effective Tradition-Bearers Communicate:

In this situation, those tradition-bearing are most likely to be heard by their opposition if they talk about the four quadrants in which order?

_____   _____   _____   _____ (answers follow)

Answer: With the same assumption that those who feel heard are more open to hearing, I suggest the tradition-bearers talk first about R-, then L+, L-, and R+.

In response to your opposition, those tradition-bearing to preserve R+ and avoid L- might say something like:

- "I hear your concerns about (read R- list). I agree that those things need to be addressed."

- "And the things you are advocating like (read L+ list) are things I think are important too."

- "When I think about those things, I wonder how we can prevent (read L- list)."

- "Because it is important to me to preserve (read R+ list)."

I hope this exercise fits whatever polarity you created. Certainly, no polarized situation is as simple as this exercise. But this can give you a feel for the sequencing of the information in the four quadrants when communicating with your opposition over a polarity. The more complicated the situation, the more important it is to determine if there are a few key polarities at the heart of the matter. If there are, seeing all four quadrants and knowing how to use them can be very helpful.

CHAPTER SIX

A Problem to Solve
or a
Polarity to Manage?

6

Why Ask?

Before discussing "how" to differentiate between a problem to solve and a polarity to manage, I will restate "why" it is helpful to distinguish between the two. The ongoing goal in Polarity Management is to stay in the upper two quadrants as much as possible. When individuals, organizations, or countries treat a manageable polarity as if it were a problem to solve, they will spend unnecessary time experiencing the downsides of that polarity. In other words, they will not manage it very well.

This rather cold, matter-of-fact statement becomes loaded with passion and power when you think of the terrible effect on people when key polarities are managed poorly. Either "Rigid" or "Wishy-Washy" bosses make work life difficult for themselves, the people who work for them, and, in the long run, for the organization in which they work. The inability of nations to manage the freedom/ equality polarity has led to horrendous suffering and recurring revolutions around the world. Some example polarities are discussed later in this book and in the supplement.

For now, I just want to be clear that it is no small contribution to an organization and its employees when a leader, together with his or her fellow workers, is able to manage key organizational polarities well. It will enhance the quality of work life and the survivability of the organization.

How Do You Know If You Have a Polarity to Manage?

If you, at least for the moment, accept the notion that it is worth determining whether you have a polarity to manage or a problem to solve, how do you figure out which you have?

There are two questions I have found useful in distinguishing between the two:

1) Is the difficulty ongoing?
2) Are there two poles which are interdependent?

I will use these two questions to highlight the difference between polarities to manage and the following three difficulties which I call "problems to solve:"

1) Either/Or Decisions

2) Mystery Problems

3) Continuum Problems

The Criteria Questions

1) Is the difficulty ongoing?

Problems to solve have a solution which can be considered an end point in a process, i.e. they are solvable.

Polarities to manage, on the other hand, do not get "solved." They are ongoing. We are always in the ongoing process of "solving" them, if you will. But they do not have a clear, end point solution. There is a never-ending shift in emphasis or focus from one pole to the other and back. Instead of saying there are problems you actually solve and some that you are continually in a process of solving, I have chosen to call the ongoing process "managing."

2) Are there two poles which are interdependent?

The solution in **problems to solve** can stand alone. Unlike a polarity to be managed, the solution to a **problem to solve** does not have the necessary opposite that is required for the solution to work over an extended period of time.

Polarities to manage, on the other hand, require a shift in emphasis between opposites such that neither can stand alone. It is a "*both/and*" difficulty. *Both* one pole *and* its apparent opposite depend on each other. The pair are involved in an ongoing, balancing process over an extended period of time. They are interdependent. They need each other. Maybe an elaboration of each type of difficulty will help.

82

Polarities to Manage

One dilemma we all manage at work and at home is PLANNING and ACTION. It might look like this:

Figure 21:
Planning/Action

L+	R+
Clear direction	Plans get implemented
Reduce mistakes	Feel accomplishment
Less waste	Learn from action
Coordination easier	Energy mobilized
PLANNING	**ACTION**
Plans not implemented	Lack direction
Lack accomplishment	More mistakes
No learning from acting	More waste
Sitting on energy	Coordination more difficult
L–	R–

The qualifying questions are:

1) Is the difficulty ongoing? *Yes.*

One can not choose EITHER planning OR taking action as a final solution. If planning is chosen as a solution and taking action is neglected, one gets the downside of planning alone:

- Plans not implemented

- Lack of accomplishment

- No learning from acting

- Sitting on energy

83

If taking action is chosen as a solution and planning is neglected, one gets the downside of action alone:

- Lack direction
- More mistakes
- More waste
- Coordination is more difficult

Thus, neither planning nor action represents a final "solution." You can never say, "We are done with this once and for all." An ON-GOING interaction between planning and action is required.

2) Are there two poles which are interdependent? *Yes.*

Though *both* planning *and* action are important, neither will function well alone. In other words, *both* planning *and* action depend on each other in order to work well. They are interdependent opposites. Planning needs action *and* action needs planning. This difficulty is a polarity to be managed because it is ongoing and it has two interdependent opposites.

Problems to Solve

Below are three types of difficulties which I call problems to solve. None of them meet the two requirements necessary to be considered dilemmas (polarities) to manage.

A) "Either/Or" Decisions

This includes a host of problems for which one has to make choices between two or more options. Who should we hire among the five applicants? To which restaurant shall we go for lunch? Or, which supplier to use? These are all what I call "either/or" decisions. We hire *either* Sam *or* Gail *or* Barbara *or* Tim *or* Tad.

An "either/or" decision-making process can easily be arranged to look like the Polarity Map. For example, in making the simple decision where to go for lunch, one could choose *either* The Spinnaker *or* El Ranchero. Each place could have one or more upsides and downsides. The Spinnaker is closer and has a more relaxed atmosphere, but it is more expensive. El Ranchero is less expensive and gives faster service, but it is further away and has a hectic atmosphere.

These opinions about the two restaurants could be put in the Polarity Map:

Figure 22:
"Either/Or" Opposites Put on a Polarity Map

L+		R+
Closer More relaxed		Less expensive Faster service
THE SPINNAKER		**EL RANCHERO**
More expensive Slower service		Farther away More hectic
L−		R−

It may look like a polarity to manage because there seem to be two opposites, each of which has an upside and a downside, but if we look at this difficulty in terms of the two criteria, we will see that it is a problem to solve, not a polarity to manage.

1) Is the difficulty ongoing? *No.*

As soon as one chooses either The Spinnaker or El Ranchero, the problem is solved. Problems of choice are solved the minute the choice is made. There is a clear sense of completion and ending rather than an ongoing balancing of the merits and demerits of The Spinnaker and El Ranchero. Some problems of choice may be extremely difficult and take considerable research and contemplation.

85

Whether to take the new job or not, whether to change suppliers or not, whether to make it yourself or buy from outside—these are all important "either/or" choices that often require lengthy consideration. Regardless of the difficulty and length of the process, when the choice is made, the problem has been solved.

Thus, *"either/or"* difficulties have a sense of finality. This distinguishes them from polarities to manage, which require an ongoing balancing of opposites.

2) Are there two poles which are interdependent? *No.*

In terms of the interdependence criteria, *"either/or"* difficulties, again, fall into the category of problems to solve rather than dilemmas to manage. The choice between *either* The Spinnaker *or* El Ranchero is a problem to be solved because the opposites do not depend on each other. One can choose either restaurant and continue to choose it forever without having to use the other one. Granted, one might want to switch restaurants to bring a little variety to one's eating; however, the decision to eat at The Spinnaker is in no way dependent upon choosing El Ranchero sometime in the future. One does not have to choose *both* The Spinnaker *and* El Ranchero.

Thus, the apparent opposites are not interdependent. You have a problem to solve rather than a polarity to manage. There is no ongoing management or balancing of opposites required.

Some have found the Polarity Map to be very helpful in making *"either/or"* decisions. They say that identifying the positive and negative aspects of each of the choices helps clarify the issue. Used this way, the map becomes a type of force field analysis. If you find the Polarity Map helpful in such a situation, I encourage you to use it that way.

Its primary usefulness, however, is in the *both/and* decisions, which I call polarities to manage. Using the map for solving either/or decisions is like using the back of a guitar as a conga drum. It works. It may even have a very resonant sound. The real potential for a guitar, however, is in turning it over and "pickin' and strummin'."

The real potential for the Polarity Map and the analytical model that it constitutes is in managing polarities well. There are plenty of problem-solving models to help you with "either/or" decisions.

Catching a Ball and Juggling

Another helpful analogy is the difference between catching a ball and juggling 3 balls. If I throw a ball to you and your job is to catch it, you have a problem to solve.

1) Is the difficulty ongoing?

With a single catch—NO:

This is a problem with a definite ending. It ends when you EITHER catch it OR it hits the ground because you have not caught it.

With juggling—YES:

Juggling is like a polarity to manage because it is ongoing. The objective is to keep one ball in the air at all times while rotating through the three balls. Managing polarities is like juggling in that you are trying to stay in the upper two quadrants on an ongoing basis.

It could be said that you have "solved" the juggling problem when you have rotated the balls through the air between your hands five or six times. I would like to suggest that, at that point, you are in the process of managing (solving) the ongoing polarity quite well. But it is not solved in any final sense. All you have to do is take your eyes off the balls for a few seconds and you will no longer be solving the problem. You will be picking balls up off the floor. At that point it is clear that you have not solved the juggling problem once and for all. You have learned to manage it better and longer than others who cannot juggle as well.

2) Are there two poles which are interdependent?

With a single catch—NO:

Once I throw the ball toward you, my job is done. There is nothing in this problem that says I must catch as well as throw in order for the problem to be solved. You EITHER catch it OR you do not.

With juggling—YES:

In juggling, the absolute interdependence of opposites is very clear. The opposites are *both* throwing *and* catching with each hand. Throwing from the right hand to the left requires an opposite action of throwing from the left hand to the right. Unless each hand is able to *both* give *and* receive balls on an ongoing basis, you do not have juggling.

A single catch is an *"either/or"* problem to solve. Juggling is a *both/and* polarity to manage.

As a leader, just think of the number of things you are "juggling" on an ongoing basis that will never be solved in any final sense. You might as well learn to juggle well and figure out a way to enjoy it.

By the way, I became so caught up in this analogy that I decided to learn how to juggle. I wanted to see what I could learn about polarity management from juggling. One thing I learned was how frustrating it was at first. But then there was a point where it all seemed to come together. I was not a great juggler at that point, but it was clear that I could do it.

I think Polarity Management is that way for some people. It is frustrating at first. There is a point, however, where it all comes together and people realize that they can identify and manage a variety of polarities. In fact, polarity management, like juggling, can be fun.

Let us move on to the remaining two types of difficulties I call problems to solve.

B) Mystery Problems

These are challenges for which one must create or discover the solution. Newton was confronted with a problem when an apple fell to the ground from a tree. Gravity was discovered and our knowledge expanded. In a Sherlock Holmes mystery, one follows the clues and tries to solve the case. How can people fly? How can things heavier than water float? Such mysteries require the ability to invent and/or discover the solutions. These mysteries are all problems to solve rather than dilemmas to manage.

In terms of the two criteria:

1) Is the difficulty ongoing? *No.*

These mysteries, which require a person to create or discover the solution, have a definite ending point. It is clearly a time for celebration when one discovers gravity, figures out "who done it," or invents the airplane. When the villain is discovered or the invention works, the problem is solved.

Many new problems may emerge from the discovery of gravity. But for the moment, there is time for celebration with the completion of a problem-solving process. We know why apples fall down instead of up. We have a natural ending when the solution is found. This definite ending of the process distinguishes mystery problems from dilemmas that need ongoing management.

2) Are there two poles which are interdependent? *No.*

When one discovers that "the butler did it," there is no need to look to the opposite of the butler in order to manage some ongoing process. When the Wright brothers flew the first airplane, they did not have to shift to the opposite of flight in order to maintain a polar balance.

In other words, we are not dealing with opposites where *both* one *and* the other must be handled properly. MYSTERY PROBLEMS are clearly problems to solve rather than dilemmas to manage. They have an end point solution and the opposite to that solution is not required in order for the solution to be effective.

C) **Continuum Problems or**
 "How close can we get to one end of the continuum given our constraints?"

This is the type of difficulty which most often is confused with polarities to manage. In a polarity presentation with a group of automotive engineers, one person expressed some puzzlement. He was working with what he saw as the heavy car/light car dilemma. He knew that considerable research had been invested in making lighter cars. His question was whether this was a crusade from the downside of heavy cars to the upside of light cars. If it were a crusade in a polarity that needed managing, he could predict some of the problems and figure out how to manage them.

It was easy to create a model in which light cars were on one pole and heavy cars on the other. It was also easy to identify the upside and downside of each. It looked something like Figure 23:

Figure 23:
Car Weight Continuum Put on a Polarity Map

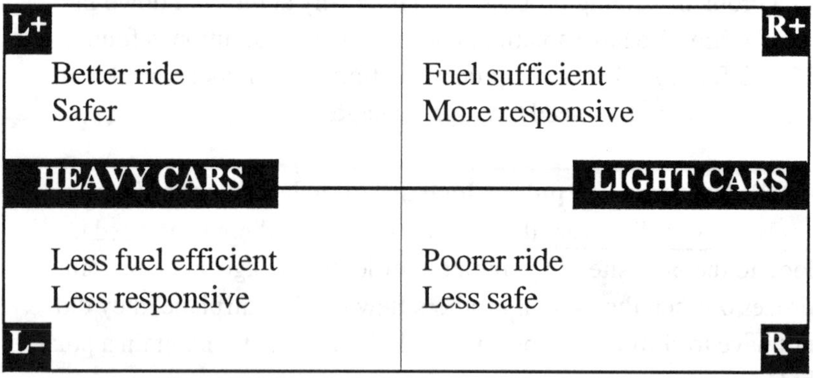

L+	R+
Better ride Safer	Fuel sufficient More responsive
HEAVY CARS	**LIGHT CARS**
Less fuel efficient Less responsive	Poorer ride Less safe
L–	R–

Though the difficulty lends itself to the Polarity Map, it is a problem to be solved and not a polarity to manage. The problem can be stated this way:

"Given our limits of time and money, how can we build the lightest car possible while adhering to defined requirements of safety and ride quality?" (There were other qualifiers we could add but the number of qualifiers does not change the type of problem with which we are dealing.)

Let's look at it in terms of the two criteria.

1) Is the difficulty ongoing? *Yes.*

In one sense, there is an ongoing quality to continuum-type difficulties. There is an ongoing effort to get closer and closer to the light car end of the continuum.

One could say that it is a problem to be solved at a given point in time. This would allow for a celebration of the car as it rolled on to the show room floor. It represents a solution to the "lightest car possible" problem for that day.

But one could say the same thing about the polarity process of planning and acting. It is possible to celebrate a plan which is the result of considerable work. It can be written up with elaborate and colorful graphs and charts, and then, like the light car, can be presented for the notice and admiration of others. Indeed, the plan is a solution to the problem, "How do we create a plan for our future?"

The "Is it ongoing?" question does not adequately help us distinguish between continuum problems and polarities to manage. Both have an ongoing quality about them. They also have points of momentary completion and celebration within their ongoing process.

2) Are there two poles which are interdependent? *No.*

The reason this is not a polarity to be managed is that one does not have to shift the focus to heavier cars in order to maintain some balance between lightness and heaviness. One can indefinitely continue to move on a continuum toward lighter cars as long as the limits of safety and ride quality are met. One is not forced to shift the emphasis to heavier cars in order to prevent negative consequences.

In other words, these opposites are not interdependent. The engineers are moving on a heavy to light continuum as far as they can.

91

At any given time, they can celebrate having solved the problem to the best degree possible at that moment.

PLANNING requires ACTION in order for the plan to have any relevance. The plan is dependent on the action. Light cars are not dependent on heavy cars. INHALING requires EXHALING in the ongoing management of breathing. Continuum problems are like dilemmas in that both are ongoing. So, we must look to the second criteria of pole interdependence to see how they are distinguishable from dilemmas to manage.

Summary

1) There are two questions which help distinguish a polarity to manage from what I call problems to solve:

- Is the difficulty ongoing?

- Are there two poles which are interdependent?

2) Polarities to manage can be distinguished from three other types of difficulties:

- "Either/Or" Decisions

- Mystery Problems

- Continuum Problems

I hope my effort to differentiate between these four types of difficulties has been clarifying. I could have identified POLARITY MANAGEMENT as a fourth type of "problem solving." You may choose to look at it that way. What is important is the ability to distinguish between POLARITIES TO MANAGE and the other three types of difficulties.

Once you know you have a difficulty which is ONGOING and has TWO INTERDEPENDENT POLES, it does not matter what you call it. Polarity Management principles will be very helpful in dealing with it effectively. To treat such a difficulty as if it had a final solution or as if one of the opposite poles is the solution will not work very well.

Exercise

Imagine yourself walking with the owner of a company from the parking lot to the front door of his business. You notice a piece of paper on the ground and pick it up as you continue your walk and morning conversation. The owner says, "Now, tell me, how do you get employees to notice things like that piece of paper and, more importantly, to pick it up?"

He continues further, "It seems like most employees just want to do what's in their job description. They overlook many of the little things that need to be done to make the place run. It's almost as if owners have different eyes than non-owners when they walk through a plant. It's not just their job, it's their place. They'll do whatever is necessary to make the place run. How do you get employees to see and act beyond the exact requirements of their job? I'd like them to have some pride and concern for the whole place."

1) Is this a problem to solve or a polarity to manage?

2) If it were a polarity to manage, what would be the two poles?

3) What is the owner complaining about (a lower quadrant)? And, what is he wishing for (an opposite upper quadrant)?

4) Now, to finish the picture, what is the upside of what he is complaining about and the downside of what he is wishing for?

5) Is the difficulty ongoing?

6) Are there two poles which are interdependent?

My responses to these questions are on the next page.

1) I think this is a polarity to manage and I would picture it like this:

L+	R+
"I will do my job." Do not interfere with others' jobs See my part	"I will do whatever is necessary for 'my place.'" Go beyond the job description to help out. See the big picture.
MY JOB	**MY PLACE**
"That's not in my job decription." Blind to needs of the place beyond the "job." Miss big picture.	Neglect own job. Interfere with other's jobs. Duplication of effort or things falling through the cracks.
L–	R–

2) The two poles are MY JOB and MY PLACE. To do MY JOB is to comply with the job description. The MY PLACE pole represents what I call "felt ownership." It is the belief that this organization is somehow mine and I will take care of it.

3) The owner is complaining about employees being in the lower left quadrant and wishing they would be in the upper right.

4) The other two quadrants are filled out in the model above.

5) Is the difficulty ongoing? Yes.

As long as you have a job, there is an ongoing need to *both* respond to the requirements of that job *and* respond to the needs of the organization which go beyond the limits of your specific job description.

6) Are there two poles that are interdependent? Yes.

A system cannot survive for long with people just performing their job to the letter. There is a need to help out beyond the specific job description. Those efforts beyond "my job description" are essential for the health of "my place."

At the same time, a system can not survive with everyone proudly proclaiming, "This is my place!" without anyone having a specific job to do. There needs to be a degree of felt ownership and a degree of job clarity for a system to function well. They are interdependent poles.

There is a downside to the effort to increase "felt ownership."

People who get overly concerned about "their place" often find themselves interfering in other peoples' jobs. That is why owners need job descriptions.

It does not work to focus on "my place" and neglect "my job." Nor does it work to focus on "my job" and neglect "my place." One does not have to be an actual owner of a business to overemphasize the "my place" pole. One can overemphasize the "my place" pole by being overly conscious of the good of the whole and getting distracted from one's job.

It is one thing to pick up a piece of paper from the ground on the way in from the parking lot. It is quite another to spend the whole morning cleaning up the parking lot when you have a job to do inside. Not only does your job get neglected, but the maintenance crew will consider it a slap in the face.

In recent years there have been some very interesting ways to enhance the "felt ownership" by employees in organizations; for example, Employee Stock Option Plans (ESOPs), involving people more in decision making, employee buyouts, etc.

In Polarity Management terms, there has been a crusade from the downside of "MY JOB" to the upside of "MY PLACE." I suggest that this important and necessary shift in emphasis is a part of a polarity to be managed and not a solution to a management problem.

CHAPTER SEVEN

How to Recognize a Well-Managed Polarity When You See One

7

Managing a Polarity Well

In this chapter I will explore polarities that are well-managed as well as those that are not. You will see common errors that result in a group or organization spending needless time in one or both of the lower quadrants (poorly managed). You will also see the essential characteristics necessary to stay primarily in the upper two quadrants (well-managed). I will use the Individual Responsibility/Organization Responsibility polarity as a case example.

Individual Responsibility and Organization Responsibility

How do you deal with members of your team who keep asking you to get the rules changed or get the structure changed so that they can do their jobs better?

On the one hand, you want to be responsive and make whatever improvements you can to help them be more effective. On the other hand, you would like to see them take some initiative and figure out how to make the most of what they already have.

As a leader, you have to do both: Challenge the organization to improve regardless of the work force and challenge the work force to improve regardless of the organization. I call this the INDIVIDUAL RESPONSIBILITY and ORGANIZATION RESPONSIBILITY polarity.

This polarity showed up most clearly in a series of management workshops at the University of Toledo, with a different set of managers coming each time from the same organization. At the end of each workshop, an evening was set aside for an open dialogue with a visiting executive. The conversation went something like this:

Manager: "It's hard to do our job when we're getting mixed messages from the top. It's even more complicated with the turnover we've had in leadership."

Executive: "That's partly why I'm here. We know there has been a problem with communication and we're working on it. I also know that communication is a two-way street. What have you done to improve the situation from your position?"

Manager: "I've tried, but I don't have much say over who the next executive is going to be or when they're going to come. What is frustrating about most of this stuff is that it's out of our control."

Executive: "You have more control than you imagine. If you get mixed messages, choose the one that makes the most sense to you and go with it. If there's something going on that is getting in the way of you doing your job, confront it. If you don't get a satisfactory response, figure out a way around it. Be creative."

This conversation could continue on and on with both the executive and the manager making valid points yet not really getting anywhere (both being accurate but incomplete).

In the middle of one of these discussions, I suggested that there was a dilemma here worth identifying. I put it on a flip chart somewhat like Figure 24.

There was general agreement that this picture described what was going on. Since the managers and the executive had received some training in Polarity Management, they quickly understood the picture and the dynamics involved. The conversation shifted and became more productive.

Now the managers and the executive started including both sides of the polarity as they made their points. A manager might say, "If upper management would just stop by on a more regular basis and with enough time to talk about what is going on, I think that would help us stay on the same track (R+). For my part, it's clear that I can take the initiative to use existing channels better than I have (L+)."

Another improvement in the discussion was that both sides of the conversation moved within the Polarity Model. For example, the executive might say, "Your point is well taken, Bill. We do need to be more responsive. That is the upside of the organization focus (R+).

Figure 24:
Individual Responsibility/Organization Responsibility

L+	R+
No waiting	Org. gets needed feedback
Tap own initiative and	Org. can respond and
creativity	improve
More org. support	More individual support
IND. RESPONSIBILITY	**ORG. RESPONSIBILITY**
Org. does not get valuable	Waiting for org. to improve
feedback	
Org. cannot respond and	Do not tap own initiative
improve	and creativity
More ind. resistance	More org. resistance
L-	R-

At the same time, the upside of the individual focus is your not waiting for us to change (L+). What can you do to carry on while I pursue these changes?"

Let us take a closer look at the diagram above (Figure 24) to understand the content and dynamics of this polarity.

The Individual Responsibility Pole

The Individual Responsibility Pole (L) represents a focus of the manager on him or herself as the source of power. The notion is "Don't do me any favors. I'll figure out a way to make a contribution, give some meaning to this job, and learn some things while I'm at it." From this perspective, individuals assume they will change and grow regardless of the circumstances in which they find themselves. They believe they can make it happen so they spend very little time trying to get others or the organization to make it happen for them. This was the focus the executive kept suggesting to the managers.

The Upside of Individual Responsibility

The upside or advantages of the Individual Responsibility focus (L+) includes:

1) *No waiting*—One can get on with it without waiting for a change in the rules, structure, or leadership.

2) *Tapping one's own initiative and creativity*—Organizational hassles and poor management are just another set of challenges to be overcome with personal assertiveness and ingenuity. This is the "I'd rather ask forgiveness than ask permission" attitude.

3) *More organizational support*—It is paradoxical that the less help we demand from our boss and our organization the more we are likely to get. There is nothing magical about this. Imagine yourself as an executive dealing with two managers. One manager, Joe, is constantly telling you he cannot do his job until you remove this obstacle or change that procedure. Your tendency after a while will be to ignore Joe as an excuse-maker.

Another manager, Judy, is trying her best to make the most of a difficult situation. She is not on your case to do this or that to make her job easier. She is the one you find yourself going out of your way to help. This help is probably given because she is trying to make do without it. Judy's efforts to make good things happen regardless of the difficulties she is experiencing will make you more receptive to her requests when they do come.

The Downside of Individual Responsibility

The downside of the Individual Responsibility pole is what happens when you ignore the need for Organization Responsibility and just concentrate on Individual Responsibility. This downside (L-) includes:

1) *The organization does not get valuable feedback*—If Judy focuses totally on her individual responsibility and does not let you know how the organization could improve to help her do her job better or improve in other ways, the organization is not getting the feedback it needs to change and grow.

2) *The organization cannot respond and improve*—Without feedback, the organization will be in trouble. The organization's practices, policies, structures, and leadership need constant attention, critical reflection, and adjustment for improvement. When individuals focus only on themselves and their jobs, the organization gets neglected.

3) *More individual resistance*—There are limits to an employee's ability to say, "I'll do my best regardless of the organization's poor policies and practices and its unwillingness to respond to my input." What was a challenge becomes a drag. The organization's lack of *response*ability leads down a well worn path from enthusiasm to apathy to rebellion.

The Organization Responsibility Pole

The Organization Responsibility pole (R) is focused on the organization's practices and policies and their effect on people's ability to do their jobs. When those practices and policies get in the way rather than help, they should be changed. Changing them in a positive manner empowers the individual and the organization by increasing the ability of both to function well. Central to Organization Responsibility is the belief that the organization can change and grow. This was the focus the managers kept suggesting to the executives.

The Upside of Organization Responsibility

The upside of Organization Responsibility (R+) includes:

1) *The organization gets valuable feedback*—To empower an organization is to give it what it needs to change and grow. To make it response*able*. One thing the organization needs is the information and wisdom that resides in the people who work there. They frequently know where the problems are and often have good ideas about how to correct them.

2) *The organization can respond and improve*—The second upside of focusing on Organization Responsibility is the belief that the organization can and will "respond" to the information by making needed adjustments.

3) *More individual support*—The more an organization takes its managers and their input seriously, the more the managers will look for ways to support the organization. Paradoxically, the more an organization, through its executives, gives the message, "We can accomplish great things with this group of managers as they are," the greater will be the investment by the managers in their own improvement and development.

The Downside of Organization Responsibility

The downside of the Organization Responsibility pole is what you get when you neglect the focus on Individual Responsibility. This downside (R-) includes:

1) *Waiting for the organization to improve*—This is what happens when individuals become "over focused" on the organizational changes necessary for them to do their job better. They lose sight of what *they* can do and the power *they* do have. They can fall into a "wait-and-see" mode which is not good for them or the organization.

2) *Do not tap own initiative and creativity*—It is a great loss to the individual and to the organization when a person looks to

the organization to "clean up its act" while not looking to themselves to rise above the challenge.

3) *More organizational resistance*—The "poor me" attitude reflected in "1" and "2" above results in the person receiving less help rather than more. The person who focuses only on Organization Responsibility and neglects Personal Responsibility is seen as a chronic complainer, and his or her ideas, which might be valuable for the organization, are ignored.

Figure 25:
Individual Responsibility/Organization Responsibility

L+	R+

No waiting
Tap own initiative and
  creativity
More org. support
	Org. gets needed feedback
	Org. can respond and
	  improve
	More individual support

IND. RESPONSIBILITY	**ORG. RESPONSIBILITY**

Org. does not get valuable
  feedback
Org. cannot respond and
  improve
More ind. resistance
	Waiting for org. to improve
	
	Do not tap own initiative
	  and creativity
	More org. resistance

L–	R–

The question is, "How do we manage this dilemma in such a way as to stay primarily in the upper two quadrants?" The organization needs feedback to improve and responsiveness to get the feedback. On the other hand, individuals need to "get on with it" without waiting for the organization to adjust to their needs.

When we, the managers and executives, talked about this dilemma, we not only experienced an immediate, mutual recognition of the issues, but also a change in the tone of our conversation. Both sides continued making their points, but they seemed to be hearing each other better. The discussion went from "either/or" to "both/and." That was certainly a good beginning.

Managing Polarities Effectively

We had accomplished 1 and 2 of the 5 elements necessary for managing any polarity effectively:

1) An awareness of the difference between a solvable problem and a polarity to be managed.
2) An awareness that there is an upside and a downside to each pole.
3) Sensitivity to the downsides as they are experienced.
4) A willingness to move from the downside of one pole to the upside of the other, knowing the process will return to the present pole in the future.
5) An understanding of the two dynamic forces involved in all dilemmas (Crusading and Tradition-Bearing). This includes an ability to be effective in Crusading, Tradition-Bearing, and mediating between the two.

Well-Managed Polarity

In a well-managed polarity most time is spent experiencing the positive aspects of one pole or the other. When the downside of a pole is experienced, it is used as a signal to move to the positive of the other pole.

For example, people who manage the Individual Responsibility and Organization Responsibility polarity well are able to challenge themselves and their subordinates to do their best regardless of the system. They are also able to challenge the system to be more responsive to them and their subordinates. They move between the two, guided by indicators such as too much waiting for the organization to

106

improve, or too little feedback from individuals as to how the organization can help. This movement is illustrated in Figure 26.

Figure 26:
Well-Managed Polarity

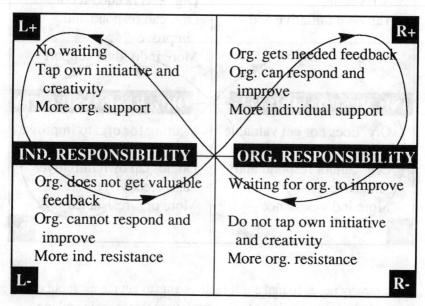

L+	R+

No waiting
Tap own initiative and
  creativity
More org. support
	Org. gets needed feedback
	Org. can respond and
	  improve
	More individual support

IND. RESPONSIBILITY	**ORG. RESPONSIBILITY**

Org. does not get valuable
  feedback
Org. cannot respond and
  improve
More ind. resistance
	Waiting for org. to improve
	
	Do not tap own initiative
	  and creativity
	More org. resistance

L-	R-

Poorly Managed Polarities

In Figure 27 (below), most of the time is spent getting either no feedback or a lot of complaining and waiting. Polarities managed this way do not flow, they flip! The picture represents a series of ineffective crusades "flipping" from one downside to the opposite downside, with very little time spent in the upside of either pole.

The "Downside to Downside" Story

Linda's employees feel like they have an unresponsive boss. She seems unwilling to advocate for them. She will not go to her boss and the other "powers that be" and tell them what kind of changes

Figure 27:
The "Flip" from Downside to Downside

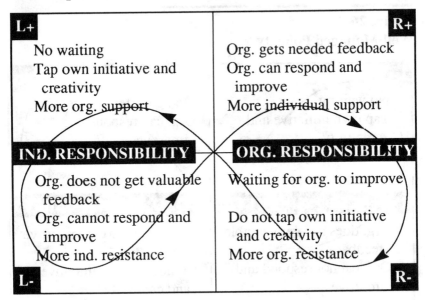

the company needs to make if it really wants to get the most out of its employees. She explains to the employees that there is nothing anyone can do and advises them to live with it. Soon she is getting little or no new feedback. Morale goes downhill until it cannot be ignored. Employee rumblings like the following can be heard: "Enough of this 'Do the best you can' stuff. When is this organization going to shape up? We can't go on like this."

The company replaces Linda with a "good listener" and "team advocate" who leads a crusade to make the organization more responsive. *A change in leadership often accompanies an effort to move from a downside in which a system has been stuck for a long time.* The crusade, neglecting the upside of Individual Responsibility and the downside of Organization Responsibility, quickly "flips" into the downside of Organization Responsibility.

The organization will stay there until the lack of individual initiative cannot be ignored and leadership tires of the organization receiving all the blame for everything that is wrong. At that point, a new leader could be brought in to lead the charge to the opposite pole. He or she will be "just what the organization needs": Someone to challenge people to grow up and take charge of their lives.

In this scenario, the crusaders eventually "win" each time by succeeding in forcing the shift to the opposite pole. But the organization loses because it experiences mostly the downside of each pole.

Both the crusaders and the tradition-bearers are responsible for the poor management of this polarity. Out of an incomplete perception, tradition-bearers resist the move to the other pole. They underestimate the downside of the present pole and the upside of the opposite pole. They keep an organization too long in one pole until it is in real trouble. This becomes a set-up to "flip" when the shift finally occurs. The crusaders promote a move which renounces any upsides to the present pole or any downsides to the opposite pole. This incomplete perception, of course, only heightens the resistance of tradition-bearers.

Remember, "crusading" and "tradition-bearing" are forces, not personality types. In Figure 27, most of the people crusading for Organization Responsibility became "tradition-bearers." Once the system shifted to the opposite pole, they would become the ones resisting the move back to the pole from which they had been crusading. In their resistance to move to the other pole they become the "tradition-bearers."

Figure 28:
Stuck in the Downside of Individual Responsibility

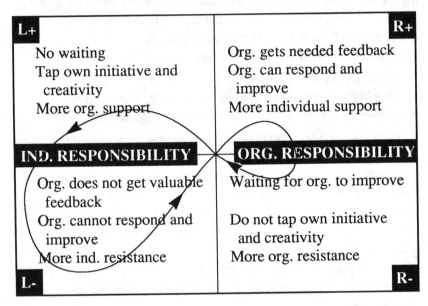

L+	R+

No waiting
Tap own initiative and
    creativity
More org. support
	Org. gets needed feedback
	Org. can respond and
	    improve
	More individual support

IND. RESPONSIBILITY	**ORG. RESPONSIBILITY**

Org. does not get valuable
    feedback
Org. cannot respond and
    improve
More ind. resistance
	Waiting for org. to improve
	
	Do not tap own initiative
	    and creativity
	More org. resistance

L-	R-

In this picture, Figure 28, the system stays stuck in the downside of Individual Responsibility, with only brief, unsuccessful efforts to shift to Organization Responsibility. In this situation, those tradition-bearing for Individual Responsibility maintain enough power to keep the emphasis on that pole. They either block those who are crusading or half-heartedly support the shift to the other pole, forcing the shift back to the original pole at the first sign of anything that makes them anxious.

The "Stuck in One Downside" Story

To parallel the previous story, let us suppose the unresponsive boss, Linda, keeps her job. On occasion, because of outside pressure or other reasons, she decides to try going to the Organization Responsibility pole and act as an advocate for her employees.

When Linda decides to shift from confronting the employees to confronting the organization, she is understandably anxious. She values "self starters" (L+) and does not want to buy into a "gripe session" (R-). That is what she is afraid will happen if she shifts to the Organization Responsibility pole. She strongly believes it probably will be a waste of time.

This hunch that it will be a waste of time is part of how those tradition-bearing set themselves up. They reluctantly go to the other pole, looking for indicators that the shift was a mistake, trying to find signs of the downside of the new pole.

So, Linda calls a meeting to hear people's concerns. The meeting is what those crusading have been asking for. But they, too, are skeptical. They are afraid nothing will really come of this meeting. They talk to each other, saying, "She isn't serious about getting the changes we need. It will just be a bunch of talk to quiet the troops, then it will be business as usual." Their hunch is that it will be a waste of time. This hunch is part of how those crusading set themselves up. They reluctantly go to the meeting looking for indicators that they are going to stay stuck in the downside of Individual Responsibility.

Notice that both the tradition-bearing forces and the crusading forces are anticipating that the shift to the other pole will not work. At the meeting, those wanting organizational changes are hesitant at first. Then they decide to test the water and see if Linda is serious. At this point, a flood of complaints comes out.

To Linda, her worst fears seem to be coming true. The meeting seems to be degenerating into a gripe session in which people just want to dump on her and upper management. No one appears willing to take any personal responsibility for any problems on the long list of complaints. She decides to take corrective action. She confronts them with how they are a part of the problem and informs them, "I didn't call this meeting just to have people dump on me and the company."

What Linda sees as balancing the conversation is read by those crusading as Linda's unwillingness to hear them out and take their concerns to the powers-that-be and get some action.

Things go from bad to worse. Everyone leaves considering the meeting a disaster. The system goes back to the Individual Responsibility pole because that is where the power is in this situation. They took a quick swing from the downside of Individual Responsibility (L-) to the upside (R+) and then downside (R-) of Organization Responsibility, followed by a quick visit to the upside of Individual Responsibility (L+) before returning, all too quickly, to where they started (L-).

Both sides are able to say, "I told you so." Both sides are able to blame the other for the disastrous meeting. And neither side is likely to see how they contributed to the mismanagement of this dilemma.

One thing is for sure—they are not likely to have another meeting in the near future where employees give input on organizational improvements. Of course, delay of such a meeting increases the likeli-

Figure 29:
Stuck in the Downside of Organization Responsibility

L+	R+

No waiting
Tap own initiative and
  creativity
More org. support
	Org. gets needed feedback
	Org. can respond and
	  improve
	More individual support

IND. RESPONSIBILITY	**ORG. RESPONSIBILITY**

Org. does not get valuable
  feedback
Org. cannot respond and
  improve
More ind. resistance
	Waiting for org. to improve
	
	Do not tap own initiative
	  and creativity
	More org. resistance

L-	R-

hood that when it does happen, it will become another dumping session.

Figure 29 is the mirror image of Figure 28. The dynamics are the same. We have the same type of "stuckness" in a lower quadrant, except this one is stuck in the downside of Organization Responsibility. In this case, you have a system in which the historic emphasis has been on Organization Responsibility and little on Individual Responsibility. The tradition-bearers, again, have the power to keep the focus on the Organization Responsibility pole. In this case, the crusaders are the ones pushing for more Individual Responsibility.

The tradition-bearers and crusaders again join forces to undermine efforts to move to the upside of Individual Responsibility. The shift to the Individual Responsibility pole has a brief touch of the upside, but the tradition-bearers (this time wanting to preserve the upside of Organization Responsibility and afraid of falling into the downside of Individual Responsibility) quickly identify indicators of the downside of Individual Responsibility and take action to pull the system back to the upside of Organization Responsibility. They are soon back to where they started.

Again, it is easy for those crusading and those tradition-bearing to blame the other for continued difficulties. Furthermore, both are unlikely to understand how they contributed to the poor management of this dilemma.

In my experience, I have found that owners and executive management tend to promote the Individual Responsibility Pole. Employees, union or not, tend to promote the Organization Responsibility Pole. If this dilemma is seen as an "either/or" problem to solve, it will become a power issue in which no matter who "wins," both will lose.

If ownership has the power and becomes unresponsive to the employees, you will get a poorly managed polarity that looks like Figure 28. If the union has the power and becomes unresponsive to ownership, you will get a poorly managed polarity that looks like Figure 29. If you get a major shift in power from ownership to union and back while retaining an "either/or" mind-set, you will get a poorly managed polarity that looks like Figure 27.

What the organization needs is the ability by those supporting each pole to see this as a polarity to manage and then to manage it well, so that the system looks like Figure 26.

Summary

1) The Individual Responsibility/Organization Responsibility polarity is an important one to manage personally. It is also important to manage as a leader of others. I know this is much easier said than done. But the job is both to challenge employees to improve, regardless of the organization, and to challenge the organization to improve, regardless of the employees.

2) Five types of skill and knowledge are necessary to manage a polarity well:

- Knowing when you have a polarity to manage rather than a problem to solve

- Knowing there is an upside and downside to each pole

- Sensitivity to the downsides as they are experienced

- A willingness to shift poles as needed

- Knowing how to talk to your opposite and mediate between opposites

3) There are such things as well-managed polarities. They are achieved by staying primarily in the upper two quadrants. When a polarity is being managed well, there is an effective alliance going on between the crusading forces and the tradition-bearing forces.

4) There are also such things as poorly managed dilemmas. Ignoring a polarity is one way to manage it poorly. The result of poor polarity management is staying primarily in one or both of the lower quadrants. When a polarity is being managed poorly, there is an ineffective alliance going on between the crusading forces and the tradition-bearing forces.

Exercise

Create a Polarity Map and diagram the dynamics of how your group moves through the four quadrants:

Think of a polarity that your work group is not managing as well as you would like. (If you need suggestions of possible polarities, see the Appendix for a list of polarities.)

1) Identify the up and downsides of each pole.

2) Put an "X" where you think your work group is right now. (Your group is, to some degree, in all four quadrants all the time. I am asking you to identify where the emphasis or energy is most concentrated at this time.)

Now, think of this polarity model with an "X" in one quadrant as one frame in the film of a movie. If you were to put the film in reverse and back it up, then start it up from six months or a year ago, what would be the path of this "X" through the four quadrants?

In which quadrant have you spent the most time? That quadrant would have the biggest loop. The quadrant where you have spent the least time would have the smallest loop, etc. The distorted infinity loop might look something like Figures 26-29.

Now think of what your group might do to keep itself in the two upper quadrants of this polarity. Make a list of some action steps. Hints:

1) Identify those who will be the ones most sensitive to each of the downsides. You might agree to encourage them to let everyone know when they are experiencing the downside to which they are most sensitive. This information will provide you with an early warning system. What you are doing is building in a self-regulating process that capitalizes on the sensitivity of different group members to each of the downsides.

2) You need to commit to the ongoing shift in emphasis back and forth and consider how that can be done.

CHAPTER EIGHT
Two Departments
in Conflict

8

Working with Key Polarities Underlying Multiple Issue Conflicts

In this chapter, I will "take you with me" to one of my consulting sessions to give you a step-by-step example of how I used Polarity Management with a client organization. It is a "How To" chapter in which I will be quite detailed about the process and the rationale. *My intent is both to make it clear and to make it easier for you to replicate or modify Polarity Management for your own use.*

The Invitation

I received a phone call from a man who said that I had been recommended to help him with a conflict situation. He headed a department at the headquarters of a Christian religious group. He went on to explain that his department and another department had been at odds with each other for some time and now the situation had become really difficult.

In an effort to clear the air and move toward a resolution, he had recently called a joint meeting at which the objective was to identify as many problems or concerns as they could. He figured that getting them out on the table would be a good first step. In half an hour of brainstorming, the two groups identified 30 problems.

At this point, they decided to go for outside help. What they had in mind was a half-day joint meeting in which they would address the identified problems. Only an organization with a history of feeding 5,000 with a few fish and a few loaves of bread would think of solving 30 long-standing interdepartmental problems in one afternoon!

They had identified a planning committee comprised of two staff members from each department, who had been elected by their peers, and the head of each department. They were to meet with an outside consultant for a few hours to plan for the afternoon conflict-resolution session.

I agreed to join them. We were not sure what could be done in half a day, but it seemed like a reasonable follow-up to the half-hour brainstorming session.

The Planning Meeting

When I got to the planning session, they already had arranged the 30 problems into categories. Each of us received a typed list. We reviewed the list for clarification and I noticed that many of the items looked more like polarities to manage than problems to solve. I told them about my interest in Polarity Management and that some of the issues between the two departments might be polarities that needed to be managed better.

They were intrigued by the idea and asked me to explain it a little more. After a brief presentation on the basics of Polarity Management, I asked them if they could see one or more of the key dilemmas that were at the heart of the list of 30 problems.

In less than two minutes, with virtually no discussion, they all agreed that the polarity was "Word and Deed." Put in other words, the people in one department were focused on communicating their beliefs (the Word) in such a way that others would also come to "believe" and would join their church. The "Word" was described as the statement of faith that one shares with others, that they may know "the Word of God" as the believer does.

"Deed" on the other hand was identified as the conduct that flows naturally from one's faith. The people from the other department were focused on their denomination's involvement in issues of service and justice. Thus, "Word" communicates the "faith through words" and "Deed," "living the faith in one's actions."

It was amazing how quickly all of the planning committee agreed that there was one key dilemma within most of the 30 problems. At this point, there was considerable interest in how to include Polarity Management as a part of the conflict-resolution afternoon for which we were planning.

Below is a summary of our plan as it was implemented a week or so later.

Theory Presentation

I began the afternoon with a presentation and discussion on Polarity Management. When everyone had some familiarity with the basic concept, I told them how the planning group had identified "Word and Deed" as a key polarity the two departments were trying to manage. Again there was relatively quick agreement that this was an important part of the dynamic between them.

Building and Working the Dilemma in Small Groups

I then asked them to get into four groups of six members. Each group included three members from both departments. The reason for this was that the two departments needed to share perceptions and understand each other better. Joint membership in the groups also would increase joint departmental ownership of results.

Each group was then directed to a place in the room where a Polarity Map was marked out on the floor with masking tape. The "Polarity Floor Map" for each group looked like Figure 30:

Figure 30:
Word and Deed

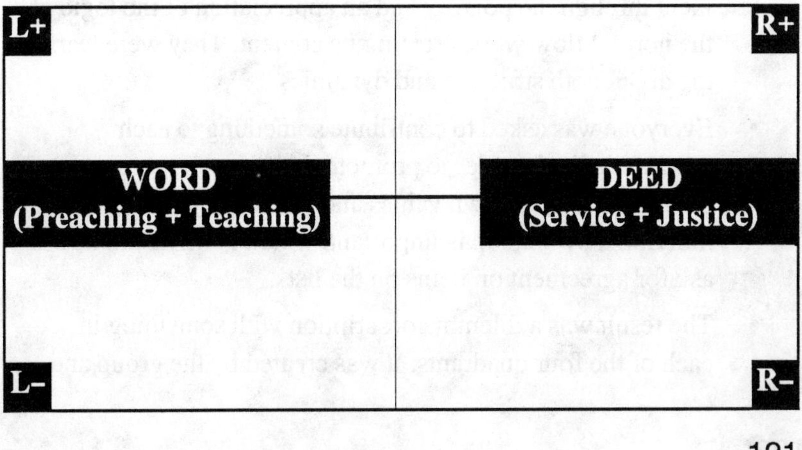

L+	R+
WORD (Preaching + Teaching)	**DEED** (Service + Justice)
L–	R–

All four groups were then given the same assignment:

Round One: "Normal Flow"

1.1   Select one person as a recorder for the group.

1.2   All six people start in (L-) and make a list of the downsides of focusing only on "Word" and neglecting "Deed." Get at least one contribution for this quadrant from each of the six members. You do not have to agree on the list. Whatever a person wants to add iss written down.

1.3   When you are through with the (L-) list, the whole group of six will then move to the (R+) quadrant. While there, make a list of those things you associate with the upside of focusing on "Deed." Again, get at least one contribution from each group member.

1.4   Continue by moving into quadrant (R-) and then (L+).

Round One Notes:

• I asked the groups to start in a lower quadrant because dilemmas tend to be driven by the energy to move from the downside of one pole to the upside of the other. One can start in either lower quadrant.

• As they moved through the quadrants in the sequence of the normal flow of a dilemma, they experienced physical movement through the polarity and an appreciation of the logic of the normal flow while creating its content. They were learning about both structure and dynamics.

• Everyone was asked to contribute something to each quadrant's list in order to promote their creating a complete polarity to fit their own values and vocabulary. Here, individual ownership is important, which is why I did not ask for agreement on items on the lists.

• The result was a dilemma description with something in each of the four quadrants. It was created by the group and

by individuals in the group so the shared ownership was likely to be fairly high.

Round Two: "Getting Unstuck"

2.1   Start again as a group in (L-). The recorder will now read the
(L-) list out loud. The other five members of the group are to
close their eyes and listen to the list. As you hear the words,
imagine yourself being in an organization in which this list
of words represents the predominant situation.

2.2   After hearing the list, your natural tendency would be to move
to quadrant (R+). But let us say in this situation that the
organization has considerable resistance to going to (R+).
That move is effectively blocked. In order to get unstuck from
(L-), move as a group to (L+). Again the recorder will read
the list while the others close their eyes and imagine being in
an organization where this list predominates.

2.3   Now move to (R-). Read the list and move finally to (R+).

2.4   When you have finished all four quadrants, stay at the site
of your polarity model and discuss your feelings and thoughts
about this exercise.

Round Two Notes:

- Round One started in (L-) and ended in (L+). Round Two
started in (L-) also but ended up in (R+). It is important for
the sake of balance that each group finish in one upper quadrant one round and in the other upper quadrant in the next
round. The reason is that whichever upper quadrant an individual or group finishes in often bears the added "weight"
of being the arrival point, as if it were the goal. A major
point of Polarity Management is that neither upper quadrant
is a final goal.

- Another reason to start in (L-) is so that people can experience the process of getting unstuck as moving in the opposite direction of the "normal flow" they just experienced in

round one. They get unstuck by acknowledging and respecting the two quadrants from which the resistance would come.

- Closing the eyes is important to cut out the distractions and enhance people's imaginations and associations with the words being read.

- Having the group discussion at the site where they have just arrived after moving through all four quadrants seems to help them recall their movements and how they felt. Often you will see people pointing and moving around as they explore what happened.

After the small group discussions, we met as a whole group to reflect on what had happened. The experience was powerful for many, which is to say that this particular polarity was important to them. More than one person reported feeling physically nauseous when they were moving from the upside of one pole to the downside of the other. Another person reported that it felt like the first time in months that they were really listening to each other. A person who had joined one of the departments a few months earlier said it felt like the first time since she had arrived that she did not have to choose sides.

Small Groups Dealing with the Issues

The next thing we did was display in large print in the front of the room the categorized list of the 30 problems. We asked people to identify one or more issues or cluster of issues that they wanted to work on for the next half hour. They were then to self-select into groups of common interests to work on these issues.

Their assignment in their working groups was to:

1) Decide which of their issues were problems to be solved and which were dilemmas to manage.

2) Prepare some recommendations for the whole group about how to move toward solving the problems and managing the dilemmas.

The group ended up with an impressive list of recommendations. They also seemed proud of not only what they had produced but how they had done it together. This is one intervention where people found Polarity Management helpful as they struggled to address the list of problems they had created.

Summary

1) Polarity Management can be useful in conflict resolution sessions if some agreement can be reached on one or a few key dilemmas underlying the conflict.

2) It does not take a long time to introduce the model and the basic principles of Polarity Management with enough clarity to be immediately useful for a group.

3) Switching from problem solving to Polarity Managing can help a group be less hard on themselves for lack of "solutions" and help them get a fresh perspective from which to manage the situation better.

4) No one is asked to contradict the accuracy of their reality, yet everyone is supported in expanding their reality. It is a significant perceptual shift from solving a series of problems to managing a few key dilemmas.

5) Physically moving as a small group through the quadrants and creating the content for each quadrant has two positive results: 1) Ownership of the picture which reflects the values and vocabulary of the members, and 2) An increased ability by everyone to see the whole picture.

Exercise

Imagine that you have both a production manager and a quality control manager working for you. They come to you out of frustration with each other. The quality control manager, Kay, says, "I just want to know if we are serious about all our talk about quality being our number one concern."

Doug, the production manager says, "Of course quality is important. But we have to keep our costs in line. We need on-time delivery to our customers and we need volume. We are going so overboard on this quality stuff that our costs in time and money are going to break us. I've got customers on my back for late shipments and our inventory is getting so low we have no flexibility for responding to the customer. The employees are frustrated because they aren't getting enough volume out the door to feel proud of their production."

Kay says, "What good is the volume if the customer rejects it? You know how frustrated employees used to be with in-house and customer rejects. Our scrap and remake rate was a disaster. I'm interested in cost reduction as much as you are. Ignoring quality won't save costs in the long run."

Here, of course, is another polarity to be managed. I was brought in to one of these conversations recently. It was a few weeks after I had made a brief Polarity Management presentation to the salary employees. It was quite clear to them that this was probably a polarity to manage and they wanted to discuss it with me.

I asked them to fill out the quadrants with what fit for them as upsides and downsides. At first they thought the two poles were quality and production. After working with it for awhile they decided it was quality and cost. The cost pole included costs in terms of money, people, and time.

You can create a cost/quality model by filling in all four quadrants. You do not need to compare your picture to mine or to one that this pair came up with. If you have some things in all four quadrants that fit for you, you are all set. Remember, shifting your collective perception from a problem to solve with two quadrants to a polarity to manage with four quadrants is a very significant step in changing the whole ball game.

If you were working with Kay and Doug, what would you want to happen in terms of their planning to manage the Cost/Quality polarity well? One suggestion is that each of them sees their job as helping the company manage this polarity well. This is different from suggesting that Kay be an advocate for quality and Doug be an advocate for cost reduction. The two of them also should listen more to each other. Though there will be a tendency for Kay to focus on quality and Doug on cost, the polarity will be managed better if they both feel some responsibility for both.

Doug's job, in terms of this polarity, is not just to reduce costs, and Kay's job is not just to improve quality. Doug's and Kay's job is to see that this polarity gets managed well. To do that they both need to become sensitive to when one pole is being emphasized at the expense of the other. This requires a fairly similar view of the four quadrants and regular, ongoing communication about how well management is going. It also requires good cost and quality measures that they both agree are the key indicators of when one or both of the poles are in trouble.

The process is overlaid with another polarity. It is important that both of them be clear and flexible rather than rigid or ambiguous. In other words, there is not a set of exact policies and procedures for managing all polarities. Knowing what they look like and how they function will provide a solid basis for you and others to create ongoing, changing processes for managing issues better than you have in the past.

CHAPTER NINE

Action Steps

9

From Theory to Application

As you go from reading about Polarity Management principles to applying them at work, this last chapter could prove helpful. Chapters Eight and Nine were examples of application with an individual and with two teams. This chapter will help you apply Polarity Management principles with a group regardless of the context in which they are working.

I begin by identifying three "Pitfalls" in using Polarity Management. They are followed by an "Action Steps" process for working with a group on a polarity of their choice.

Three Polarity Pitfalls

1) *Polarity Management as the "Answer" to Everything*

> "If all you have in your tool kit is a hammer, everything looks like a nail."

Sometimes people get caught up in the fact that polarities really are everywhere. But not all polarities are worth attention. Furthermore, *there are a whole host of problems that need to be solved.* Polarity Management is just one helpful tool in what should be a very sizable leader's tool kit.

2) *Avoiding the Issue*

> "We cannot solve it, so let's forget it."

Polarity Management can be misused as yet another excuse for not addressing those issues we want to avoid. I have received reports from groups using Polarity Management that some members identify an issue as a polarity which cannot be "solved" and therefore imply that it should be ignored.

131

Such an assumption is directly contrary to Polarity Management Principles. If it is a polarity to be managed, like "individual and team," ignoring it does not mean it will go away. As long as you have a team, the "individual and team" polarity is being managed. The only question is "How well?" Ignoring it just reduces the possibility of managing it well. The result of managing it poorly is that individual team members and the team as a whole will spend unnecessary time in the downside of one or both of the poles.

Ignoring the "individual and team" polarity implies that, since it is not a solvable problem, there is nothing you can do about it. In fact, Polarity Management is built on the exact opposite assumption: *Polarities function under a set of principles which, when understood and acted upon, can dramatically increase our ability to manage them well.* When managed well, the individual team members and the team as a whole will spend most of their time in the upsides of the two poles.

3) *No Decisions*

> "If it is not a problem to solve, there are no decisions to be made."

Sometimes people see problem solving and decision making as the same thing. From that perspective, if the problem is unsolvable, there are no decisions to be made. On the contrary, managing a polarity well requires ongoing decision making based on an ever-changing reality.

For example, here are a few decisions which are made on an ongoing basis while managing the "individual and team" dilemma:

1) What do we need to do to keep us in the upper two quadrants?
2) At this point in time how do we measure team performance and give recognition to the team for good work?
3) How do we measure individual performance and give recognition for it?

132

4) How do we know when it is time to shift the focus from one pole to the other?

5) How do we communicate most productively with those who want to focus on team when we want to focus on the individual?

We are always involved in many polarities. We cannot give all of them our complete attention. Some we manage with little or no attention, like breathing. To others, like "individual and team," we may give considerable attention until we build in ongoing processes for measuring and recognizing good work and identifying problems at both the individual and the team level. At that point, the "individual and team" polarity may be managed with relatively minor effort.

You need to make decisions regularly about which polarities to attend to and how. We often are helped in identifying dilemmas either by someone crusading for a change and/or by someone concerned about losing something important and tradition-bearing to avoid a problem.

Indecision happens when one gets "caught on the horns of a dilemma." In this situation, there seems to be equal power and equal validity to opposing views. No decision in this case is a decision in favor of inertia (things at rest tend to stay at rest and those in motion tend to stay in motion). If those crusading have sufficient momentum for change in the organization at the time of "no decision," they probably will override those who are tradition-bearing. In which case, "*no* decision" is in fact a decision in favor of those crusading. If there is little or no momentum for those crusading, "no decision" is in fact a decision in favor of those who are tradition-bearing. The problem with these decisions, which appear to be indecision, is that you are much more likely to get the downside of the pole of whichever side "wins."

If an organization is stuck in a struggle between those crusading and those tradition-bearing, an important consideration is "How long has the system been emphasizing the present pole which the tradition-bearers want to maintain?"

The longer the emphasis has been on the present pole, the more important it probably is to shift the emphasis. Also, the deeper will run the roots of that tradition. This means recognizing the upsides of the historical pole becomes more important, though harder to do.

Summary

Polarity Management is one tool among many that are helpful for a manager doing her or his job. It can be over-used and misused just like any other management tool. It is an over-use to apply it to problems which can and need to be solved. It is a misuse to use it as an excuse for avoiding issues or not making decisions.

Exercise

Polarity Management "Action Steps"

Here are the action steps of Polarity Management. Check your understanding of the basics of Polarity Management by applying these steps to a dilemma that requires managing.

1) IDENTIFY—The polarity

   - Agree on a polarity you want to manage better.

2) DESCRIBE—The whole polarity

   - Agree on at least the four quadrants.

   - Find neutral words for the poles. This may help "bridge" the up and downsides if you are having trouble filling in a quadrant.

3) DIAGNOSE—Critical Elements

   - In which quadrant is the system located now?

   - Who is crusading? (Name individuals or groups.) What are they critical of? (The answer is in one of your lower quadrants.) What are they promoting? (The answer is in the diagonal upper quadrant from where you found your last answer.)

   - Who is tradition-bearing? (Name individuals or groups.) What are they afraid of losing? (The answer is in the other upper quadrant to which you have not yet referred.) What are they afraid the crusade will lead to? (The answer is in the lower quadrant you have not referred to yet.)

4) PREDICT—Problem Anticipation

   - Where will the resistance to those crusading for change come from? (Note those you identified as tradition-bearing and the quadrants on which they will be focused.)

135

- What will happen if the crusading group "wins" and the concerns of those who are tradition-bearing are neglected? (See the quadrant below the one to which those crusading want to go.)

- What will happen if the tradition-bearing group "wins" and the concerns of those who are crusading are neglected? (See the quadrant below the one which those tradition-bearing want to preserve.)

Notice that once you have a complete picture in front of you, it is quite easy to diagnose and predict from the picture.

5) PRESCRIBE—Guidelines For Action

- Actions for those crusading—Acknowledge the concerns of those tradition-bearing:

    — Clarify what you value and do not want to lose from the pole that those tradition-bearing are trying to protect.

    — Let those tradition-bearing know that you are aware of the downsides of where you want to go and that you want to guard against those downsides.

    — Think of assurances you can give those tradition-bearing that you do not intend to "throw the baby out with the bath water."

- Actions for those tradition-bearing—Acknowledge the concerns of those crusading:

    — Let those crusading know that you are aware of the downsides of the pole which has been emphasized recently, and that you, too, would like to reduce those downsides.

    — Clarify what you value and want to gain from the pole to which those crusading want to go.

— Think of assurances you can give those crusading that you are interested in "changing the bath water."

- System Policies And Practices—Managing This Dilemma Effectively

    — What communication systems need to be in place to alert the system when it slides into one of the downsides?

    — What additional system practices would be in place if this polarity was being well-managed (moving back and forth with relative ease and staying primarily in the two upper quadrants.)? What steps could you take to move in that direction?

This process may seem quite elaborate, but you can move more quickly through the steps as they become more familiar. The part of the process where you might slow down at first is the System Policies and Practices step. Do not get discouraged if that does not get addressed right away. Exploring policies and practices can come with time. As you and your group come to understand the dynamics of Polarity Management, this process will get more efficient.

Conclusion

My conviction is that polarities (dilemmas, paradoxes, inter-dependent opposites) are everywhere, in our work-lives and in our personal lives. We do manage them, some better than others. It is my hope that Polarity Management will provide a basis for an additional perspective on our dilemmas and skills in managing our polarities. They won't go away. Managing them poorly can be extremely costly to individuals, organizations, and nations.

Managing them well, on the other hand, can be extremely enhancing for our lives individually and for the systems in which we live. It is this possibility of life-enhancement which excites me and humbles me at the same time. I hope you find it useful.

Resources

Additional Resources

1) SUPPLEMENT—The most immediate resource on Polarity Management is the following seven-part supplement containing more application examples and more principles of Polarity Management.

2) POLARITY APPLICATIONS GROUP—If you would like more information on Polarity Management training and materials, you can contact the Polarity Applications Group through the University of Toledo. (See page 144.)

3) Eight fine books loaded with examples from business and industry on the importance of managing opposites are:

BEYOND RATIONAL MANAGEMENT—Mastering the Paradoxes and Competing Demands of High Performance, by Robert E. Quinn. Jossey-Bass, 1988.
This is a great management skills development book, focusing on eight key roles that all leaders perform in organizations. These roles also represent eight key functions all organizations need to perform well. The eight roles are laid out as four pairs of opposites. The author provides assessment material to determine your relative strength in each of these roles and skill-building exercises to help you on "The Road to Mastery" as a leader.

THE LEADERSHIP EQUATION—Leadership, Management, and the Myers-Briggs, by Lee and Norma Barr. Eakin Press, 1989.
Clearly the most researched set of polarities are the four pairs of preferences in the Myers-Briggs Type Indicator. The authors' premise is that "... a balanced individual style will produce leadership enhancement." They do a great job of looking at the four pairs of preferences in leadership terms. They identify the "strengths and weaknesses" (upside and downside) of each and give solid recommendations for how to "develop more balance" (manage the polarity better).

141

THE CHARACTER OF ORGANIZATIONS—Using Jungian Types in Organizational Development, by William Bridges. Consulting Psychologists Press, 1992.

The four Myers-Briggs preference pairs are used to identify an organization's "character" the same way they are used to identify an individual's "type." Polarity Management blends well with this book as Bridges looks at how an organization's life cycle requires an ongoing shift in emphasis from one set of preferences (pole) to another. Change and Transition are also looked at in terms of managing opposites.

A FORCE FOR CHANGE—How Leadership Differs From Management, by John P. Kotter. Macmillan, 1990, and *MIND OF A MANAGER, SOUL OF A LEADER,* by Craig R. Hickman. John Wiley & Sons, 1990.

These solid books both differentiate between two sets of opposites which are essential for organizations to flourish. One set of skills and orientations are classified as those of a "manager," while the other set are seen as those of a "leader." Kotter focuses on the many ramifications of what I call the Stability and Change Polarity, while Hickman has 43 brief chapters, each focusing on a different polarity within the Manager/Leader framework.

MANAGING ON THE EDGE—How the Smartest Companies Use Conflict to Stay Ahead, by Richard Tanner Pascale. Simon and Schuster, 1990.

This great book is about "cultivating and harnessing tension." Pascale identifies seven pairs of "contending opposites" (Polarities to Manage) which function best when they are in dynamic, constructive tension. The seven polarities are integrated by relating all of them to one central pair of extremes: "overcontrol" and "chaos." In Polarity Management terms, these extremes are the two downsides of the key polarity that needs to be managed.

THE TAO OF LEADERSHIP—Leadership Strategies for a New Age, by John Heider. Bantam Books, 1985.
This wonderful little book is adapted from Lao Tzu's book: *Tao Te Ching* (Book of How Things Work). The book is full of opposites and the value of paying attention to them. It is written in very easy to understand language, yet is loaded with insights and perspectives for, as the author declares, "anyone who aspires to a leadership position."

NECESSARY WISDOM—Meeting the Challenge of a New Cultural Maturity, by Charles M. Johnston, MD. ICD Press, 1991.
This is an expansive book for those who want to explore a whole series of polarities that go beyond a strict management focus. Dr. Johnston explores areas including health, the cosmos, ethics, peace, love, and truth.

Polarity Applications Group

The Human Resource Development Center (HRDC) at the University of Toledo is the clearing house for research, development, consultation and training in Polarity Management. Barry Johnson is working with a group of people from inside and outside the University, called the Polarity Applications Group.

This group of professionals is dedicated to making Polarity Management available to as many people as possible. To that end, we are eager to work with you and your organization.

We are available to provide consulting and training either at your organization or at the University of Toledo. We also will provide updated materials for training and research.

We would greatly appreciate from you:

1) Any questions you have about Polarity Management or its application.
2) Examples of your efforts at applying Polarity Management and what you learned from them.
3) Suggestions for improving our training or our materials.

We believe there is considerable room for development, especially in the area of diverse applications. If you are interested in collaborating with us in research and development, or in any other way, we welcome your interest.

THE POLARITY APPLICATIONS GROUP
Human Resource Development Center
University of Toledo at SeaGate Centre
401 Jefferson Avenue
Toledo, Ohio 43604
419-321-5150

Supplements

The main text provides a fairly brief overview of the basics of Polarity Management. This supplement continues the process. A variety of new polarities are used to explore additional principles. Each section of the supplement is written to stand on its own. Thus, you can pick and choose which sections you want to read and in what order. The only exception is that it will be helpful to read Section E before F or G.

OUTLINE AND SECTION SUMMARIES

Section A—An Owner and a Manager Struggling with Change

This application is based on the case of an owner who claimed she wanted change and a manager who found her resisting his efforts at change. The polarity discussed is Stability and Change. The One Pole Myth is identified and explained. The exercise examines the Product-Driven/ Market-Driven polarity.

Section B—"Tough/Love" in the Workplace

This section addresses the issue of measurement, its importance, and its limitations. The polarity includes Conditional Respect, which is measurement-based (Tough), and Unconditional Respect, for which measurement is irrelevant (Love).

Section C—How "Participatory Management" Gets Into Trouble

This section looks at the group and organization levels of the company system. Two often confused polarities are contrasted to highlight their differences: 1) Autocratic Management/Participatory Management, and 2) Centralized Decisions/Decentralized Decisions.

Section D—The Joys of Stress and Tranquility

This section gives you a chance to look at stress in your work and personal life from a Polarity Management perspective.

Section E—Generic Polarities

This section describes "Generic Polarities." There are some generic polarities that have many "sister" polarities. All sister polarities, regardless of whether you are talking about a work group or the United Nations, have the same content in the four quadrants of their Polarity Maps. This means you can transfer learning from a small system to a large one, and vice versa.

Section F—Values: The Art and Science of Polarity Management

This section deals with issues at the national and international level. Apartheid is probed as part of a polarity, and we see how the content of our Polarity Map is dependent on our values. At the same time, the dynamics of the polarity we create are independent of our values. The Merged Pole Myth is also discussed.

Section G—Capitalism and Socialism

This section shows how these two socio-economic orientations tend to parallel the Individual/Team polarity. Thus we have a Polarity Management perspective on evolutionary and revolutionary change at the national and international level.

SECTION A

An Owner and a Manager Struggling With Change

Crusading For "Change"

Clearly, one recent emphasis in management has been on change. Everything is seen as in flux. As a leader you are told that you must learn how to deal effectively with change or your organization will not be able to compete. Because you are also told that "people resist change," you need to figure out how to manage this resistance in order to make needed changes.

These points are accurate and incomplete. In Polarity Management terms, they are the basis of a general "crusade" toward the upside of CHANGE. This crusade is a part of the polarity of STABILITY and CHANGE. From this polarity perspective, we automatically have some clues about how to be effective with this issue. One thing we know is that the more one pole becomes emphasized, the more important it is to not lose sight of the other pole. AS YOU FOCUS ON CHANGE, IT IS IMPORTANT TO VALUE STABILITY.

Does This Owner Want Change Or Not?

I was meeting with an owner (call her Gail) and the senior, general manager for her system (call him Tom). The discussion was about the mixed messages Tom was receiving from Gail and from four other owners about whether they really wanted change or just liked to talk about it.

Background History

Two years earlier, Tom had been asked to leave his job as manager of one of the three companies in the system in order to create a fourth company. The new company would provide coordination and service functions for the other three. The new company would also spearhead the drive toward diversification for the system as a whole.

This plan involved considerable change in a system that had been quite stable and comfortable in the past because it was protected by

151

proprietary products and consistent market demand. Tom was to be accountable to Gail in this process. She assured him that she and the other owners were completely behind the change effort and that he would be fully supported. He was to do whatever was needed to make the transition.

Tom was a good choice to lead the reorganization process. He had risen through the ranks in Gail's companies and knew the existing system. He had respect at all levels, had an ability to see the "big picture," was willing to take risks, and loved a new challenge. He had also been warning the owners about their mature products and encouraging them to diversify. He believed in the moves they wanted to make. In spite of their stated support, however, Tom kept noticing resistance to some of his change efforts. It was coming from both owners and employees.

I suggested to Gail and Tom that we might look at their issue in terms of a polarity to manage. Both Gail and Tom had some familiarity with Polarity Management. They agreed to take a look and found it easy to fill in the quadrants on a flip chart. Figure 31 (below) is their picture of the situation.

They agreed on naming the polarity STABILITY and CHANGE. They elaborated on what they meant by the STABILITY or CHANGE of PRODUCTS, PERSONNEL, and PROCEDURES. When they shifted to the four quadrants, they started with the upside of CHANGE (R+). You could see Tom's excitement being re-kindled as they listed: NEW ENERGY; NEW PERSPECTIVES; NEW CHALLENGES, which included the gaining of NEW SKILLS, KNOWLEDGE, and EXPERIENCES; and finally, a statement which Tom saw as very important to include, WILLING TO TAKE RISKS.

The opposite of this attractive list was the downside of STABILITY (L-), whose quadrant they filled out next. They labeled it STAGNATION, and it included: NO NEW PERSPECTIVES, NO NEW CHALLENGES, and UNWILLING TO TAKE RISKS.

Figure 31:
Stability and Change

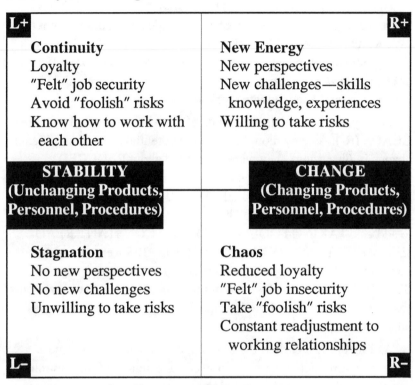

We then filled in the upside of STABILITY, which they labeled
CONTINUITY (L+). Tom had taken the lead in identifying the upsides of CHANGE and now Gail took the lead with the upside of
STABILITY. LOYALTY and "FELT" JOB SECURITY were the
first to come to her mind. Due to the stability of the companies there
were some long-time employees who had shown a lot of LOYALTY
to the owners and their organizations. This was clearly a plus that
Gail valued. They listed "FELT" JOB SECURITY rather than real
job security because both Gail and Tom knew that real job security
in their system was dependent upon making some significant changes. Employees feeling secure that the companies had a future and

153

that they had a future job with the companies was considered a "plus."

Gail was clear about the need to AVOID "FOOLISH" RISKS while making needed changes. She also made an important point that "We KNOW HOW TO WORK WITH EACH OTHER." The continuity of leadership and followership helped them be more efficient as experienced work teams. They knew each other's strengths and weaknesses and knew how to work well with each other.

Finally, we went to the downside of CHANGE, which they called CHAOS (R-). As they thought about the potential costs of significant change in the system, they were concerned about REDUCED LOYALTY. There had been some employee turnover and they were hearing comments that indicated "FELT" JOB INSECURITY was becoming a serious problem. They knew it was an issue they needed to address. TAKING FOOLISH RISKS and CONSTANT READJUSTMENT TO WORKING RELATIONSHIPS were two more downsides which emerged naturally as opposites of the upside of STABILITY. Thus, in about ten minutes, they were able to agree on some content for each of the four quadrants. Now the question was how to manage it better.

As I mentioned earlier, their system of companies had some proprietary products. The protection of the patents and the continued demand for their products tended to keep the organization more on the STABILITY pole (L). As usual, it was the experience of the downsides of that pole (STAGNATION) that had prompted the owners to encourage Tom to lead the move toward diversification and reorganization. They wanted the benefits of NEW ENERGY, NEW PRODUCTS, and NEW PERSPECTIVES.

When we looked at the situation from the Polarity perspective, it helped us understand some of the dynamics of the past two years. They agreed that the system and the owners, regardless of their words, tended to emphasize the stability pole. They also agreed that Tom had not received the degree of support he had expected when he was encouraged to make needed changes.

Gail said, "We seem to make timid efforts to go from the downside of STABILITY (L-) to the upside of CHANGE (R+). Then, with the slightest indication of instability, we get afraid of CHAOS (R-) and pull Tom back toward the STABILITY pole. We end up spending too much time in the downside of STABILITY (L-)."

Figure 32:
Power with Tradition-Bearers for Stability

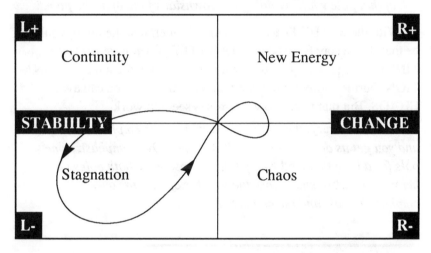

Here we have an example of the second type of poorly managed polarity I described in Chapter Seven. This is one in which those tradition-bearing for STABILITY hold significantly more power than those crusading for CHANGE, and so the system stays primarily in the downside of STABILITY.

Then Tom looked a little puzzled. "Something else is happening which doesn't seem to fit with Gail's description," he said. "We are starting to experience more CHAOS (R-), but it isn't coming from an overemphasis on CHANGE. It seems to be coming from all the STAGNATION (L-) we fell into with the overemphasis on STABILITY. I thought by focusing on STABILITY (L), you could avoid CHAOS (R-). But that's not what is happening."

155

Tom was having an important insight into a common and understandable mistake in thinking about polarities. I call it the One Pole Myth.

The One Pole Myth

The ONE POLE MYTH is:

"If you stay on one pole, you will get the upside and downside of that pole while avoiding the downside of the opposite pole."

With the STABILITY and CHANGE dilemma, the myth would be that if you stay focused on STABILITY you at least get CONTINUITY even though you may have to put up with some STAGNATION. Furthermore, by focusing on STABILITY, you can avoid CHAOS. But that is not how dilemmas seem to work.

On the contrary, *the one pole reality is: over-emphasize one pole and you get its downside (move A-B below). Over-emphasize one pole for a long time and you get the downsides of both poles (B+C below). You also tend to lose the benefits of both the over-emphasized pole and the neglected pole.*

Figure 33:
The One Pole Reality

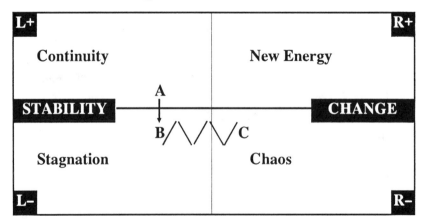

Do you know the old truism that our fears are often self-fulfilling prophecies? That is what is going on with this myth. The paradox is that those who are deeply afraid of the downside of change end up experiencing the downside of change. Their fear results in an over-emphasis on stability and neglect of the need for the upside of change. The resulting stagnation, if experienced long enough, under-mines LOYALTY as people wonder if the organization is really going anywhere. There is "FELT" JOB INSECURITY as people ex-perience the lack of NEW PERSPECTIVES and the lack of NEW CHALLENGES. Desperation can set in and people who had been UNWILLING TO TAKE RISKS end up TAKING FOOLISH RISKS. The result of fearfully clinging to the STABILITY pole is first the downside of STABILITY, then eventually, the downside of CHANGE as well. NOTHING BREEDS CHAOS LIKE STAGNA-TION.

The same basic problem can develop on the other side of the polarity. The fear of stagnation results in the overemphasis on change and neglect of the need for the upside of stability. One can then become stagnated in chaos.

In each case, YOU GET WHAT YOU ARE AFRAID OF BY CLINGING TO ITS APPARENT OPPOSITE. This is what Gail, Tom, and their system of companies were dealing with. It explains how they could be experiencing the downside of change even though they were spending most of their time at the stability pole.

What To Do?

So what do you do when you find yourself like Tom and Gail, in a no-win situation? They had been involved in a one pole focus and were getting the downside of both poles. The first thing to do is recognize that you have a polarity to manage. Second, you must agree on the content of the model. The third is to agree on the recent dynamics within the model, i.e. in which quadrant have we been spending most of our time lately? The fourth is to identify who is tradition-bearing and who is crusading. Then those crusading and those tradition-bearing can negotiate ways to keep the dilemma in the upper two quadrants rather than the lower two.

As you will recall, it is often helpful to reverse the normal flow through the quadrants to get a polarity unstuck. In this case, it was important for Tom to be clearer about his support for CONTINUITY and other upsides of STABILITY (L+). He also would let Gail and the other owners know he had considered the possible downsides of various change efforts (R-) when he made proposals and reports on progress. This would help assure them that he was not TAKING "FOOLISH" RISKS.

It was clear that Gail was tradition-bearing for stability and that Tom was crusading for change. Because of the history of the stability pole, Gail agreed to make every effort to stay with change efforts and not "pull back" or undercut the process every time she grew anxious about the downsides of change (R-). She reconfirmed that she really did not want to be stuck in STAGNATION (L-) and was eager to get on with the needed changes (R+). Gail and Tom went through the above steps in about twenty minutes.

They further agreed to discuss the stability and change dilemma at the next owner/manager retreat. The discussion went well at the retreat, and I believe this polarity will be managed better in the future. Although there are no final solutions to managing a dilemma, I hope this gives you some clues about how to improve its ongoing management.

One final comment. Risk is often associated with the CHANGE pole of the STABILITY/CHANGE polarity. This was true of the discussion with Gail and Tom. I suggest that STABILITY is as risky as CHANGE. What is risky is emphasizing either pole to the neglect of the other.

Summary

1. It can be helpful to identify popular trends in the culture or in business which are "crusades" within a polarity to be managed. The "trends" often occur as a correction from a pre-

vious focus on the opposite pole. When the trends are seen as a solution to a problem rather than as a needed shift in emphasis within a polarity, the polarity will not be managed well.

2. The present emphasis on change and the managing of change in business and industry is part of a polarity to be managed. The polarity is STABILITY and CHANGE. From the perspective of the polarity model, the push toward change can be seen as a crusade of real importance. You will be more effective in leading change efforts if they are seen in the context of the larger picture, which includes both stability and change.

3. There is a One Pole Myth which comes from either/or thinking. The myth is: If you stay in one pole, you can keep the benefits of that pole, minimize the downsides of that pole, and avoid the downsides of the opposite pole. The One Pole Reality is: If you stay in one pole long enough, you lose many of the benefits of that pole, increasingly experience the downsides of that pole, and find yourself experiencing some of the downsides of the opposite pole. In other words, staying in one pole out of fear of the downside of the other pole paradoxically results in your getting what you were afraid of.

4. When you are experiencing the downsides of both poles, it could mean that you have been stuck in one pole for quite awhile. Determine which pole it is, identify all four quadrants, then get clear about the upside of the pole you have been stuck in and the downside of the opposite pole. These two quadrants are the source of the "stuckness." By identifying and dealing with these two quadrants you are reversing the normal flow to get unstuck.

5. The notion that "People resist change" is accurate but incomplete. People resist the downside of change (chaos) and the loss of the upside of stability (continuity). It is also true that people resist the downside of stability (stagnation) and the loss of the upside of change (new energy).

Exercise

CASE STUDY

Below is the essence of an actual discussion by a group of five owners planning their direction for the future. As they were looking at their system of companies, the question came up as to whether they were to be product-driven or market-driven.

I suggest you read the discussion and imagine yourself as a part of the group. See if you can identify the upside and downside of the polarity they are managing. (These owners were all women so I will use fictitious women's names.)

Cheri: "I think we are product-driven and ought to stay that way."

Jan: "I disagree. We are market-driven. At least we had better be if we want a future. We cannot afford to lose touch with the customer. We'll end up making products that no one wants."

Cheri, "Yes, but we make very special products with great added value and we take great pride in that. Besides, I don't want us running around chasing the customer. We'll end up losing track of our niche and do things we've no business doing."

Ruth: "I agree with Jan. Look at what happened to the major automotive companies in this country. They got all caught up in themselves and lost contact with the customer. They ended up making cars that no one wanted. Then along came the Japanese who did a better job of listening to the customer. They took a big chunk of the market."

Carol: "But Cheri has a good point. What about 'sticking to our knitting?' We have manufacturing operations. Are we going to become a travel agency just because tourism is up? If we spend all our energy listening to the customer, we are going to get out of touch with ourselves, with what we do best, and what we want to do. Doesn't that count for anything anymore?"

Jan: "You can have all the pride you want in your product. If the customer doesn't want it, you're in trouble. We may not go into the tourism business but we better be out there listening to what the customer has to say about alternative products because the ones we're making aren't going to last forever."

This debate could have gone on for some time. What proved helpful in this situation was identifying the issue as a polarity to manage rather than a problem to solve. Since the women were familiar with Polarity Management, showing them the model with the four quadrants filled out shifted the whole conversation. The fifth owner, who had been silently listening, proposed a direction for the future which included the upsides of both the product- and market-driven. It had become clear to everyone that either focus without the other would not work.

Assignment*:

1. Based on the above conversation and your own thinking about this polarity, fill out the four quadrants of the "Product-Driven and Market-Driven" polarity below:

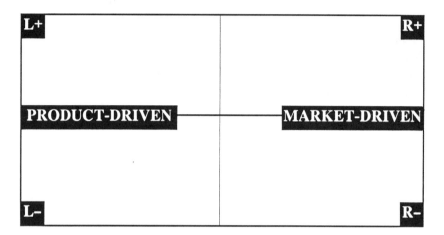

2. Write a brief statement of direction for this system of companies in relation to product and customer, including the upside of both poles:

*Possible options on the next page.

Possible content for the Polarity Model of this dilemma:

L+	R+
Pride in our product Doing what we do best Listening to ourselves— knowing our limits	Listening to the customer Make what customer wants/ needs Being customer-responsive
PRODUCT-DRIVEN	**MARKET-DRIVEN**
Out of touch with the customer Make products customer does not want	Loss of pride in product Doing what we do not do well Out of touch with ourselves— over-extended, "Who are we?"
L–	R–

Possible Statement:

> We are a manufacturing organization with great pride in our
> products and services. We are highly customer-responsive
> without losing sight of our strengths and limitations.

SECTION B

"Tough/Love" in the Workplace

Tough Love

"Tough Love" has been a popular term in recent years. It conveys the dual message of being "no nonsense" on the one hand (Tough) and being "caring" on the other hand (Love). In this section we will look at a larger, underlying polarity of which "Tough/ Love" is a part: Conditional Respect (Doing) and Unconditional Respect (Being).

A central focus of this polarity is the issue of measurement. As a leader, you have no choice but to measure. At the most basic level, you measure whether people show up for work or not. You measure your income and your expenditures and hope the former is greater than the latter. The question with measurement is not "Do I measure?" but: 1) "What do I measure?" 2) "How do I do it?" and 3) "What do I do with the results?" Although these questions are all very important, even if you had good answers to them, you still would have only the Conditional Respect pole of the picture. Of equal importance is the Unconditional Respect pole for which measurement is irrelevant.

Conditional Respect *(Doing)* and Unconditional Respect *(Being)*

I saw a quote on a sweatshirt the other day that summarized this polarity very well:

TO DO IS TO BE — Socrates

TO BE IS TO DO — Plato

DO BE DO BE DO — Sinatra

Polarity Management includes all three. In other words: Doing is important; Being is important; and it is important to move easily between the two.

An effective leader knows both how to show respect based on performance *and* how to show respect regardless of performance. One is conditional: It depends on what the employee (peer, boss) is *doing*. The other is unconditional: It is based only on the fact that the person exists. It is based on their *being*.

Conditional Respect is earned by doing and built on the measurement of performance. Unconditional Respect cannot be earned by doing. Earning is not required. It is a birthright. It cannot be lost. Measurement is not needed.

In Figure 34 we can see the content of the whole polarity. I will discuss the content of the two upper quadrants first, and then briefly look at the two lower quadrants.

Figure 34:
Conditional Respect (Doing) and
Unconditional Respect (Being)

L+	R+
People Respected for What They Do	**People Respected for Who They Are**
Measurement used to: 1) Recognize good work 2) Identify problems and make improvements 3) Develop consequential thinking	Recognition of our equality as human beings People listened to regardless of status
CONDITIONAL RESPECT **(Earned by Doing)** *(Measurement needed)*	**UNCONDITIONAL RESPECT** **(Given Freely)** *(Measurement not needed)*
People Are Simply a Means to Organization Profits	**People Lack Accountability for What They Do**
People as objects of measurement—valued only for what they can do for the company People only a "number," "cog," and resent it	No measurement: 1) Not recognizing good work 2) Not identifying problems and making improvements 3) No consequential thinking
L–	R–

168

The Upside of Conditional Respect (L+): People Respected For What They Do.

Conditional Respect has at least three main contributions. Each is dependent on some form of measurement.

1) Conditional Respect recognizes good and improved work.

All accomplishments and the celebration of accomplishments are dependent on some form of measurement. It is impossible to effectively recognize a person for good or improved work without first having measures in place which he or she respects.

Think of the last accomplishment you had at work that you felt proud of. Got one? Notice that some measurement was involved and that the measurement was one that you respected. It does not matter whether the measurement was yours or someone else's as long as you think it is legitimate. *If you do not respect the measurement system, you will feel no pride or sense of accomplishment from its results.*

We need Conditional Self-respect. That is called pride in our work. We also need Conditional Respect from others. That is called recognition for our work.

Recognition for good or improved work is one of the most powerful options a leader has for improving both morale and productivity. And, the Behaviorists are right. YOU CANNOT RECOGNIZE GOOD OR IMPROVED WORK WITHOUT RESPECTED MEASURES IN PLACE.

2) Conditional Respect identifies problems and makes improvements.

The first contribution of conditional respect is that you know when you are doing well and can celebrate it. The second major contribution is that you know when you are not doing well and can do something about it.

This is the accountability part of Conditional Respect. If you do good work, you receive respect. If you do not do good work, you do not receive respect. If you do not come to work, you do not get paid. If your work performance is inadequate, the performance will be addressed and some improvement plans will be made. If you do not improve, you will have to find other work.

This may sound cold and uncaring to Unconditional Respect advocates, but it is an extremely important part of the upside of Conditional Respect. There *is* a conditional side to life. We do not do anyone any favors by pretending that is not true. By overly protecting people from the negative consequences of their poor work, we overly endanger the company and, therefore, everyone's work. We also remove the possibility of them earning pride in their work (Conditional Self-respect) or recognition from others for their good or improved work.

Without measurement, it is impossible to identify problems and take corrective action. It is important to point out that there is no choice about whether to measure or not. The choices are in what to measure and what to do with the results.

3) Conditional Respect develops consequential thinking.

This third upside to Conditional Respect is an outgrowth of the first two. *Consequential thinking is developed only by experiencing consequences.* The consequences may be seen as positive or negative. What is important is that we have consequences in our lives. That is the basis for our sense of power.

The ability to affect our lives and the lives of others by our actions can be very empowering. The message is: "My life and my actions are of some *consequence.* I can and do have an effect on my life and the lives of those around me."

All consequential thinking is based on some measurement. It is the measurement of our effect. From the perspective of developing consequential thinking and empowerment, being told my work is unsatisfactory and why is much better than getting no information on my work.

When we do not hold employees accountable for their work, whether good or bad, we are disabling them by not developing their consequential thinking, and it is an indicator to them that we do not care about them. This is a reasonable conclusion from the Conditional Respect point of view. From this perspective, if you cared about me, you would let me know whether my actions were increasing your Conditional Respect for me or not. Not to let me know means my actions are irrelevant to you and that, therefore, I am irrelevant to you.

This is why the Conditional Respect pole of the polarity is so important. It is essential in terms of caring for people. It is also essential in terms of caring for the company. Concern for the "bottom line" is a part of the Conditional Respect pole.

The Upside of Unconditional Respect (R+): People Respected For Who They Are

There is a type of respect that can be given freely without fear of bankruptcy. When you walk into a new job as a manager, you do not have to look at everyone's performance chart before you say hello and show people some respect. They deserve that because they exist. They do not have to earn it. The respect comes from their being, not from their doing.

This kind of respect is most easily understood in terms of our relationships with our children. For example, when my children come home from school with their report cards, I do not have to see their report cards to decide if I love them. My love is not conditioned by how they are doing in school. I love each of them for who they are. I know I love them before seeing their report cards. I also know I will continue to love them regardless of what their report cards say. In terms of my love for them, the report card is irrelevant. My love is not performance-based. In that sense, it is unconditional.

Unconditional Respect, like unconditional love, is not performance-based. It can be neither earned nor lost by doing. The emphasis on Unconditional Respect is growing in many organizational settings. In recent years, there has been a whole new spirit of cooperation between Union and Management, with a strong trend toward showing respect for *all* employees.

The United Auto Workers and General Motors have launched an impressive program called Quality Network. In their summary of the process they write of CUSTOMER SATISFACTION *THROUGH PEOPLE,* which has five key elements:

- Inviting the people of GM to be full partners in the business
- Recognizing people as a corporation's greatest resource
- Demonstrating commitment to people
- Treating people with respect
- Never compromising integrity

Notice how the emphasis is on the upside of Unconditional Respect. When organizations talk about respect for ALL employees, they are talking about something employees should get by virtue of BEING an employee. It is not performance-based. The message is not "We will show respect to those employees who rate 80% or higher on our performance standards."

Let me share another statement signed by a group of people demanding Unconditional Respect.

"We hold these truths to be self-evident, that all men (people)* are created equal, that they are endowed by their creator with certain unalienable rights, that among these are life, liberty and the pursuit of happiness."
— *Declaration of Independence of the United States of America*

This declaration assumes that there is a list of certain birthrights which belong to all people and which idealistically cannot be taken away. Whatever is on that list belongs in the upper right quadrant, for it is the upside of Unconditional Respect.

---

*(The signers were white men demanding this Unconditional Respect for themselves. Women and people of color have been making their own demands for unconditional respect. Over the past 200 years we have moved toward the reality of a Declaration of Independence which could read, "...ALL PEOPLE ARE CREATED EQUAL,...")

You and I may disagree on what should go on the list of "unalienable rights," but one thing we both know is that this upper right quadrant will not be empty. There is such a thing as Unconditional Respect. It is harder to get a handle on than the upside of Conditional Respect, but it is no less important or less powerful a factor in the process of managing.

As I mentioned before, Conditional Self-respect is called pride in my work. Conditional Respect from others is called recognition for my work. There is a parallel on the Unconditional side. UNCONDITIONAL SELF-RESPECT IS CALLED PERSONAL DIGNITY. UNCONDITIONAL RESPECT FROM OTHERS IS CALLED A RECOGNITION OF MY HUMANITY.

Like all polarities, if you emphasize one pole to the neglect of the other, you will get the downside of that pole. Let us look at the two downsides.

The Downside of Conditional Respect (L-): People Are Simply a Means to Organization Profits.

There IS a downside to Conditional Respect. It can be overlooked by those who highly value its good points.

In 1968, in Memphis, there was a strike by garbage workers. A picture in the paper that day showed a worker on the picket line with a sign that read simply, "I AM A MAN!" Notice the sign does not say, "$.30 MORE PER HOUR." That would be a demand for respect for his labor, which would be Conditional Respect.

This man was demanding Unconditional Respect. It was the kind of respect he felt he deserved as a human being. It was the kind of respect he was not required to earn by measuring up to anyone's standards. It came as a birthright. It was an "unalienable right" proclaimed by the authors of the Declaration of Independence.

There are some indicators that you have moved from the upside to the downside of Conditional Respect. Employees talk about being mistreated. And they may not be talking about wages and benefits. They could be frustrated with how they are talked to and how they are not listened to. You hear comments such as "It's not what she says but how she says it that gets to me." Employees begin to feel like they are only a "number" or a "cog." They do not feel valued as human beings, but as objects of measurement only valued for what they can do for the company. They resent this.

When the situation becomes too impersonal and the respect too conditional, pressure emerges for "respect for all employees."

If the response is too little or too late, work slows down and people start carrying signs that say, "I am a person."

They become crusaders for Unconditional Respect.

The Downside of Unconditional Respect (R-): People Lack Accountability For What They Do.

The primary fear of people who resist the move from the Conditional Respect pole to the Unconditional Respect pole is the fear of losing accountability. Their fears are well-founded and need to be acknowledged and dealt with. Focusing only on Unconditional Respect and neglecting Conditional Respect leads to a lack of accountability and a lack of credibility.

In the lower right quadrant of Figure 39, we can see the opposite parallels to the upper left.

1) **Without standards of measurement, there can be no recognition of good work.**

If I want to tell an individual or a team that they are doing a great job, such a statement needs to be based on some sort of performance measurement. If it is not based on some measurement, I lack credibility.

I have walked through plants with well-meaning owners and managers who, as they went along, praised every employee for doing a great job. Praise is only effective if warranted. An employer must have some basis for making complaints. If there is none, the workers will know it. They have their own standards for determining who is doing good work and who is not. If someone who has been doing poor work is complimented by a manager in the same way as some-

174

one who has been doing good work, the compliment loses its value to both workers. Furthermore, the manager's credibility becomes undermined. It is this kind of "glad handing" that managers who advocate Conditional Respect see as dishonest.

The problem is not with honesty or intent. The problem is with language. The leader accused of glad handing is often using conditional respect language to convey an unconditional respect message, and it does not work. The unconditional respect message is something like, "I want you to know I respect you and care about you as a person." That message is better conveyed by *listening* to employees regardless of their performance and by actions which demonstrate concern for all employees.

Unconditional respect alone is a disaster. The lack of standards with which to recognize good and improved work is its major downside. And with no measurement, any recognition for good work will, at best, earn a manager the image of being a nice, naive person.

Without standard measures, there is no good work, no recognition of good work, no celebration of good work, no sense of accomplishment and no pride in one's accomplishments.

2) Without standards of measurement, there can be no identification of problems and making improvements.

How do you help employees improve their work? This is impossible without measuring their present performance levels. This is the accountability issue. With no measures, no one is accountable for what they do or do not do. Those of us who tend toward the Unconditional Respect side avoid confronting people with poor work. We tend to ignore the value and importance of Conditional Respect and imply that Unconditional Respect is more beneficial for people than Conditional Respect. This perspective interferes with our managing this dilemma well. Workers get away with things they should not and, as I indicated earlier, they can see the lack of accountability as a lack of caring.

The whole notion of "continuous improvement" is built on the assumption that you have worthwhile standards in place. These indicate whether the situation is improving or getting worse. Without indicators that you have minor problems, you end up with major problems that you cannot ignore.

Those of us who advocate Unconditional Respect tend to avoid measuring performance levels because we believe in respecting people regardless of their performance, and because the results could be negative. We do not like confronting poor performers. We do not like to stand in judgement of others. And we tend to avoid firing those poor performers who do not improve enough to keep their jobs. We would rather be "understanding."

3) **Without standards of measurement, there will be no conse-**
   quential thinking.

Whether the consequences are positive or negative, if I do not experience any consequences I will not develop consequential thinking. One of the major complaints I hear from managers is the lack of accountability in their organization. They make comments such as "After people have been around here 8-10 years they can just coast. There is no way they will ever be fired regardless of how much they slack off"; and "Young people these days seem to think everything should come to them just for showing up! They do not seem to think they have to earn their promotions."

This irresponsibility and unaccountability is in part due to over-protection and lack of consequential thinking. In the workplace, it is possible, in the name of respect, for people to get away with conduct which is not good for them or for the company. Poor work habits and poor performance are tolerated, and everyone loses.

Sometimes this happens when unions get very strong and over-protect their members. At other times the over-protection comes from owners or managers who really do care about the employees and the employees' families, and this concern is translated into a toleration for nonsense from the employees.

When this happens, you are experiencing the downside of Unconditional Respect. It is a disaster. Hard-working employees resent workers who are not "pulling their weight" and they resent management for not dealing with them. This over-protective situation is not good for the poor performers, either. Their poor performance needs to be addressed so that a problem-solving process which has a chance of improving work performance can take place. Without such a process, employees are denied the opportunity for the pride and recognition that can come from good or improved work.

Another complaint I often hear is "Nobody seems to notice when you really do a good job. The only time anyone gets any attention is when they goof up." This problem has to do with an unbalanced type of measurement. Not recognizing good work is just as disabling as not addressing poor work. In both cases, the result is a lack of consequential thinking. The message is the same: "What an employee does or does not do is irrelevant." There clearly is a downside when you focus on Unconditional Respect to the neglect of Conditional Respect.

Union/Management Negotiations

In all Union/Management negotiations, both kinds of respect are demanded by both sides. On the surface, the negotiations appear to be about pay for labor. And they are. That is the Conditional Respect side, which depends on measurements like dollars per hour and health insurance benefits.

But negotiations are also about Unconditional Respect. Although Conditional Respect is absolutely essential, it cannot stand alone. Without the addition of Unconditional Respect, it becomes mechanical and impersonal. Those negotiators who do not know how to show Unconditional Respect will find themselves struggling unnecessarily over all sorts of conditional issues. The notion is something like this: "If you do not show respect for me as a person in our negotiations, I will make you pay (for this lack of Unconditional Respect) by being even more demanding in terms of the conditions of the contract (Conditional Respect)."

Leaders with only Unconditional Respect are more likely to "give away the store." Leaders with only Conditional Respect are more likely to have a walk-out. One type of respect without the other is like trying to snap your fingers without your thumb.

The trade union movement was based on the right to negotiate the measures of Conditional Respect. The measures, whatever they turn out to be (wages, benefits, etc.), are part of the Conditional Respect pole. The right to negotiate itself is a part of the Unconditional Respect pole. Whether in a union shop or not, the dilemma of Conditional and Unconditional Respect is always being managed.

Why Not Celebrate What We Do *AND* Who We Are?!

On the conditional side of life, we celebrate our accomplishments and our doing, which is important. On the unconditional side of life, we celebrate life itself, our being alive and a part of creation. This also is important. In terms of celebration, think how ridiculous it is to assume that we have to choose one or the other. Why not celebrate both? As a matter of fact, in terms of Polarity Management, you cannot have one without the other. It is difficult to celebrate who we are if we have not done anything. It is also difficult to celebrate what we are doing if we do not respect who we are.

Summary

1) There are two kinds of Respect: Conditional and Unconditional. Not only are both important in working with people, they are interdependent opposites, a Polarity to Manage. This polarity provides a context for understanding both the importance and the limitations of measurement.

2) Measurement of performance is the basis for Conditional Respect. Measurement is essential for recognizing good and improved work, identifying problems and making improvements, and developing consequential thinking.

3) The other type of respect is Unconditional. It comes to us at birth and cannot be earned or lost. This respect comes to us for "being." Measurement of performance is irrelevant. Your effectiveness as a leader will increase as you improve your ability to show both Conditional and Unconditional Respect.

Exercise

These are some questions you may find interesting to ask yourself:

- Which pole of the Unconditional Respect/Conditional Respect polarity do I lean toward?

- What examples in my work life indicate that I tend to favor that pole?

- How has that preference been a strength for me at work?

- Do I have an example of when I overemphasized that pole and experienced some of the downside consequences?

Here are a few suggestions for demonstrating Conditional Respect:

1) *With the employees,* identify key individual measures to indicate if they are doing good or improved work. Watch the measures and give recognition to individuals when good or improved work is indicated.

2) *With work groups,* identify key group measures to indicate if they are doing good or improved work. Watch the measures and give recognition to work groups when good or improved work is indicated.

One essential element is that you identify the basis for the recognition, i.e. the conditions for the Conditional Respect. For example, a person or group could have increased production by x% with no loss in quality. You may come up with a variety of ways to show recognition.

What are some other ways you might show Conditional Respect?

Here are a few suggestions for demonstrating Unconditional Respect:

1) *Listen and seriously consider what is being said.* For example, in the process of creating measures for Conditional Respect, listening to all employees for their input rather than just listening to top performers.

179

2) *Drop by to see people and talk to them about how they are doing as people with families, joys and concerns.* These conversations are not about performance. They are about life and how it is going for you and for them.

What are some other ways you might show Unconditional Respect?

SECTION C
How Participatory Management Gets Into Trouble

Two Management Trends

The Polarity Management map and principles are useful in under-standing trends or "fads" in management. Often these trends are shifts in emphasis from one pole to another. Two recent shifts have been: 1) Toward Participatory Management, and 2) Toward Decentralized Decision Making. In this section we will look at both of these trends as crusades within two different polarities. One polarity is AUTOCRATIC MANAGEMENT/PARTICIPATORY MANAGEMENT; the other is CENTRALIZED DECISIONS/DECENTRALIZED DECISIONS. We will use these two polarities to understand some of the ways Participatory Manage-ment gets into trouble.

Autocratic/Participatory

The general crusade toward the upside of Participatory Manage-ment comes from some legitimate criticisms (downsides) of Auto-cratic Management and legitimate visions of the advantages (upsides) of Participatory Management. From what has already been discussed in this book, identifying Participatory Management as half of a polarity to manage gives us a quick reading on some potential problems and how to deal with them. We know, for example, that those who see Participatory Management as a solution to an either/or problem will not manage this polarity very well. They will generate unnecessary resistance from those who are tradition-bearing and will tend to see them as an opposition to overcome. If they ignore the wis-dom of the tradition-bearers and manage to overwhelm them, they will end up all too quickly in the downside of the Participatory Management pole.

When this happens, we know the fault will not be with Par-ticipatory Management. The difficulty will stem, in part, from seeing it as a "solution" in the first place. This perception will become the basis for calling Participatory Management a "mistake" later on. Let us take a look at the four quadrants in Figure 35.

Figure 35:
Autocratic/Participatory

L+	R+
Decisive Efficient (short term) Clear responsibilities	**Support for Decisions** Group wisdom used Synergy Enthusiasm
AUTOCRATIC	**PARTICIPATORY**
Lack of Support for Decisions Lack group wisdom Lack of synergy Lack of enthusiasm	**Indecisive** Inefficient (short term) Unclear responsibilities
L–	R–

The crusaders who promote PARTICIPATORY MANAGE-MENT want to move toward the SUPPORT FOR DECISIONS (R+) that you can get when people participate in the decision making. They also want the benefits they can get from GROUP WISDOM, SYNERGY, and ENTHUSIASM when everyone feels involved and important. At the same time, they are also trying to get away from the opposite set of circumstances which they have experienced, the downside of AUTOCRATIC MANAGEMENT (L-).

The tradition-bearers who resist this move do so with good reason. They believe in being DECISIVE (L+). They know it is more EFFICIENT, at least in the short run, and they like the advantages of CLEAR RESPONSIBILITIES. They want to avoid the opposite set of circumstances (R-), which they fear will happen if the organization dabbles in this PARTICIPATORY MANAGEMENT stuff.

I have consulted with some organizations where Autocratic/ Participatory Management has been seen as an "either/or" struggle.

When those crusading for Participatory Management win, the organization tends to experience INDECISIVENESS, INEFFICIENCY and UNCLEAR RESPONSIBILITIES (R-). When those tradition-bearing against Participatory Management win, the organization tends to experience LACK OF SUPPORT FOR DECISIONS, LACK OF GROUP WISDOM, LACK OF SYNERGY, and LACK OF ENTHUSIASM (L-). When the downside of the winner's pole becomes a problem, whoever lost can say, "I told you so." And they do.

Sometimes I consult with organizations on the rebound. They have tried Participatory Management and are struggling with its downsides. A new crusade is stirring to return to a more autocratic management system (go from R- to L+). Those who had been victorious crusaders for Participatory Management are now tradition-bearing to stay on that pole and "work out the kinks." They do not want to return to an autocratic situation and its downsides, which they still remember vividly.

Seeing the issue as a polarity to manage rather than a problem to solve will help in dealing with it effectively. The group will need to see the whole polarity and assess the upsides of both poles. Then it will be necessary to pay attention to when, on the one hand, group members experience too much indecision or ambiguity about responsibilities, or when, on the other hand, they make decisions that go unsupported. These downside indicators can be used to shift the emphasis back and forth in an ongoing management which allows the system to get the best of both poles.

But there is another important polarity which needs to be addressed before we go any further with this one.

Centralized Decisions and Decentralized Decisions

The second trend I mentioned was toward decentralized decisions. I suggest that we need both centralized and decentralized decisions and that either alone will not work well.

What I mean by centralized decisions is that decision making is retained by a leader or by the group as a whole, and therefore, retained at the center of authority. What I mean by decentralized decisions is that decision making is delegated away from the leader or the group to an individual or subgroup, and therefore, delegated away from the center of authority.

According to these definitions, it is possible to have an autocratic system which is very *decentralized* because the leader *delegates* most of the decision making to others. If the leader in an autocratic system *retains* most of the decision making, it will be a *centralized system.*

At the same time, it is possible to have a participatory system which is very *centralized* because the group *retains* most of the decisions itself. A participatory system can be *decentralized* when the group is willing to *delegate* decisions to individual members or to subgroups.

From this perspective, "participatory" and "decentralized" are not the same thing. You can have one without the other. Decentralization of decisions is essentially a delegation process. In considering that process, I have found it helpful to look at decision making on a continuum rather than "Either I'm in on the decision or I'm not." Decisions, like many other things in life, are not that black and white.

The Decision Continuum

Usually efforts at Participatory Management are made within a larger system which has a hierarchy of bosses and subordinates. Even when there is a concerted effort to reduce the number of layers, some form of "flattened" hierarchy remains. The emphasis on participation usually means pushing the decision making DOWN to the lowest level possible. This is a very important first step. The second step is equally important: the group that has received authority to make decisions needs to push the decision making one step further by delegating OUT to individuals and subgroups. Let us first look at pushing decisions DOWN, then we can look at pushing them OUT.

Pushing Decisions Down

Figure 36 is a continuum for decisions that you might make with a group that is accountable to you. Let us say that this group is composed of six people, including me. This continuum has the five types of possible decisions about which we had agreed to keep each other informed. The arrow on the right indicates the desire to push decisions down.

Figure 36:
Hierarchical Decision Continuum with You as Group's Boss

Type 1) No talking — You decide and tell group	
Type 2) We talk — You decide and tell group	Centralized
Type 3) We talk — We decide	
Type 4) We talk — Group decides and tells you	
Type 5) No talking — Group decides and tells you	Decentralized

My assumption is that there is a time and place for each of these five types of decisions. As our boss, if you wanted a lot of control, you could have 90% of the decision making correspond to Type 1 or 2. In that case, you would either 1) decide without talking to us and let us know your decision, or 2) we would discuss the issue so you could get input from us, then you would decide and tell us your conclusion. Your lack of delegation would result in a quite centralized decision-making process.

187

If you wanted to push the decision making down, you might shift to some Type 3 decisions in which we talk over the situation and then decide together. I would also identify this as a centralized decision-making process in that I, the subordinate, still cannot act without clearing the decision with you and the group. Remember, I am defining the degree of decentralization as the degree of freedom for autonomous action based on delegation away from centralized authority. When you and the group talk and decide together, you have given up some autonomous decision-making control by delegating it to us, but I have not gained any autonomous decision-making control; I still cannot decide on anything without "our" agreement, which requires your agreement, and that of the rest of the group. Thus, a Type 3 decision still has centralized control although the center has shifted from you to you and the group.

If you wanted to push the decisions down farther, you could have a decision-making processing like that of Type 4 or 5. In that case, you would either (4) talk with us so you could have your input and then we would decide, or (5) not talk with the group about it at all. The group would make the decision and keep you informed. In this case, your high degree of delegation would represent a more decentralized decision-making process. Decision Types 4 and 5 are shaded to help set them apart as one pole, while decisions 1, 2, and 3 fit on the other pole of the Centralized/Decentralized polarity. We will get to the polarity map shortly.

Notice that 2, 3, and 4 are similar at the start. They all begin with "We Talk." This is a great source of frustration in decision making, for misunderstandings can occur.

We could be talking about an issue, with you believing we are having a Type 2 discussion. You therefore think we are providing input for you to consider, and that the final decision is yours to make alone.

The group, on the other hand, thinks we are having a Type 3 conversation. We hear each other out and believe we will make the decision together. Later, you meet with us and tell us your decision and we are upset because we thought we had made a different decision together earlier. From the group perspective (Type 3 decision), you have broken our agreement. From your perspective (Type 2 decision), you could easily be surprised. You do not remember an ironclad agreement on a decision. You remember telling us our ideas had real merit and seemed like a viable solution. But you were just getting input from us and others, not making a decision at that time.

As a leader, I encourage you to be clear when you are in a "We Talk" situation as to whether it is a Type 2, 3, or 4 conversation. This mis-communication happens all the time. Fortunately, this is not a difficult issue to clear up if everyone is aware of the continuum. All someone has to do is ask, "What type of decision-making process are we in as *we talk* about this issue?"

In your relationship with the group, it will be helpful if you and the members have a mutual agreement that all five types of decisions are okay and then are clear on which type you are using at a particular time.

In terms of pushing decision making down, let us say there are a large number of decisions that you are delegating to our group as Type 5 decisions, which we are to make and keep you informed of. Now you have done the first step: PUSHED THE DECISION MAKING DOWN. The next step is one the group has to do: PUSH THE DECISIONS OUT.

Pushing Decisions Out

In Figure 36, we were looking at a hierarchical relationship with you as the group's boss. Thus it was a 1–5 top down model of delegation. Once the delegation reaches the group, the group becomes the center of authority and now must decide which decisions it wants to delegate to individuals or subgroups. This new arrangement is represented in Figure 37.

Figure 37:
Decision Continuum on Concentric Circles
with Group as Boss

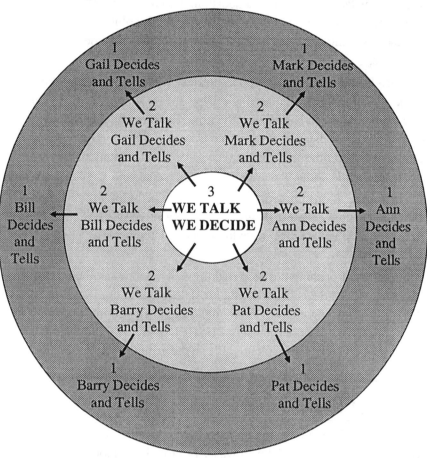

Each ring represents another level of delegation empowering the individual to act without clearing the action with the group. Decision Types 1 and 2 are shaded and are in the decentralized pole of the Centralized/Decentralized polarity. Decision Type 3 is in the centralized pole. The arrows represent the desire to push the decisions out from the center.

As groups try out Participatory Management, they often assume that 90% of the decisions will be Type 3 (We Talk—We Decide). They also often assume that being in on the decisions will be personally empowering. Type 3 decisions are empowering primarily to the group. What is empowering to the individual are Types 1 and 2, in which the individual can decide and act without clearing it with the group.

No work group can survive with 90% of the decisions being Type 3. It is too centralized. There will be too many meetings and the group will not be able to provide its goods or services. What the group needs to do in Participatory Management is to appreciate the tendency to have everyone in on all decisions and constantly resist that tendency. This is necessary in order to give the participatory experiment some chance of success. In other words, PARTICIPATORY MANAGEMENT GETS INTO TROUBLE BY BEING TOO CENTRALIZED.

The group needs to delegate to its individual members the authority and responsibility to make decisions. This means, of course, that each individual in the group will not be a part of most decisions. IT IS BY LETTING GO OF THE EMPOWERMENT ANTICIPATED FROM BEING IN ON ALL DECISIONS THAT YOU GAIN THE EMPOWERMENT TO MAKE YOUR OWN, INDIVIDUAL DECISIONS. The group needs to empower its membership and empower itself by good management of the Centralized/Decentralized (Keeping Authority/Delegating Authority) polarity.

Type 3 decisions are needed only on key issues where group wisdom and long-term support are important. Only about 5% (pick any small number) of the decisions would be Type 3. Though few in number, these decisions are the crucial ones. Another 15% to 20% would be Type 2. The remaining 75% to 80% (pick any large number) would be Type 1.

The effort to push decisions out will be resisted. The resistance will come from 1) THE DESIRE TO BE IN ON ALL DECISIONS and 2) FEAR OF THE BURDEN OF INDIVIDUAL MISTAKES.

Let us look at these two resistances to decentralization from the group.

1) The desire to be in on all decisions

When people have been in centralized, autocratic systems, one of their main frustrations is "not being in on the decisions." This frustration is greater the longer the person at the top retains decisions and refuses to delegate.

When an organization shifts to Participatory Management, people assume that they will finally be part of the decision-making process. In the new, participatory system, *everyone* wants to be in on *all* the decisions.

This is a set-up for disaster. You find the whole office staff sitting around discussing the shape of the water cooler when, in fact, no one cares about the shape of the water cooler! What is primary for them at this point is participating in the decision. What the decisions are about is secondary. IT IS EASY TO UNDERESTIMATE HOW IM-PORTANT IT IS FOR PEOPLE THAT THEY BE IN ON DECISIONS, ANY DECISIONS, WHEN THEY HAVE BEEN LEFT OUT IN THE PAST.

I consulted with a mental health agency in which virtually everyone was in strong support of the concept of Participatory Management. The director shared her frustration with me: "It seems like every time I turn around, someone is complaining to me about not being included in a discussion before a decision was made. They say things to me like, 'I thought this place was different. I thought you were serious about participation in decisions, but this seems like the same old stuff.' I'm not sure what to do. There is no way we will be able to get anything done if everyone has to be in on every decision."

She was right. What was happening was that staff members were holding firmly in their hands the new-found right to be "in on the decisions." Anything that smacked of a denial of that right was cause for complaint. The content of the decision was not the issue, it was the right to be included in the process. HANDLING THIS DESIRE

FOR INVOLVEMENT IS AN IMPORTANT PART OF ANY PAR-
TICIPATORY MANAGEMENT EFFORT.

2) Fear of the burden of individual mistakes

There is another reason to want the decisions to stay in the group.
Group decisions protect the individual and the group from individual
mistakes. If someone has been in a highly centralized, autocratic system for a long period of time, they are not well prepared to take on
personal accountability for making wrong decisions. This is especially true if the centralized, autocratic system was intolerant of mistakes.

Even if there is no history of punishment for one's mistakes, if a
person is not used to taking on authority and responsibility for
decisions, the prospect of making a mistake can be frightening. The
fear may not be of personal consequences. An individual could be
afraid that his or her independent decision could be a mistake that
hurts the group or the organization. Keeping all decisions in the
group and taking advantage of "group wisdom" is a way for individuals to protect themselves and the group from their individual
mistakes.

A number of years ago, a group of us started a manufacturing
operation which had no hierarchy and no job descriptions. Outsiders
counseled us that we needed to build in safeguards to make sure individual members weren't out there making bad individual decisions
that would ruin the young company. What we found was not that
members were running around making all sorts of organization-
threatening decisions. On the contrary, the problem was how to get
each of us to feel free to make some decisions without checking
everything with the group. The fear was not of punishment but of
making a bad decision which we might not have made if we had run
it by the group first. We soon learned that we had to make more individual decisions and that each of us and the group could learn from
our mistakes. HANDLING THIS FEAR OF INDIVIDUAL MIS-
TAKES IS ANOTHER IMPORTANT PART OF ANY PAR-
TICIPATORY MANAGEMENT EFFORT.

These two forces lead to the over-centralization of decisions in most Participatory Management efforts. In order to give the effort a chance, it is helpful to see the whole polarity and to respect these two resistances to decentralization. Figure 38 is a map of the Centralized/Decentralized polarity as it might look within a Participatory Management setting.

Figure 38:
Centralized/Decentralized Decisions in a
Participatory Management Setting

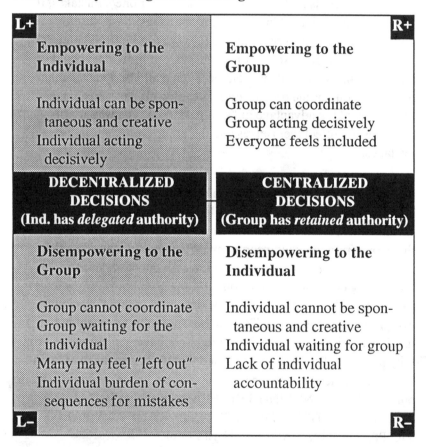

L+	R+
Empowering to the Individual	**Empowering to the Group**
Individual can be spontaneous and creative Individual acting decisively	Group can coordinate Group acting decisively Everyone feels included
DECENTRALIZED DECISIONS (Ind. has *delegated* authority)	**CENTRALIZED DECISIONS** (Group has *retained* authority)
Disempowering to the Group	**Disempowering to the Individual**
Group cannot coordinate Group waiting for the individual Many may feel "left out" Individual burden of consequences for mistakes	Individual cannot be spontaneous and creative Individual waiting for group Lack of individual accountability
L–	R–

The Decentralized Decisions pole is shaded and corresponds to the shaded areas in Figures 36 and 37.

DECENTRALIZED (Delegated) DECISIONS can be very EMPOWERING TO THE INDIVIDUAL (L+). If they have the freedom to decide on a particular issue, they can be more SPONTANEOUS and CREATIVE. They are also able to be more DECISIVE. At the same time, with total DECENTRALIZATION, it can be DISEMPOWERING TO THE BOSS OR THE GROUP (L-). They CANNOT COORDINATE and find themselves WAITING FOR THE INDIVIDUAL. Another downside is that MANY MAY FEEL "LEFT OUT" of the process and resent it. Also, when the individual makes the decision, he or she is left with the BURDEN OF CONSEQUENCES FOR MISTAKES.

CENTRALIZED (Retained) DECISIONS can be very EMPOWERING TO THE GROUP (R+). They can perform the COORDINATION of effort and ACT DECISIVELY on those decisions they do not delegate. Another bonus is that EVERYONE FEELS INCLUDED. At the same time, total CENTRALIZATION can be DISEMPOWERING TO THE INDIVIDUAL, who will lose SPONTANEITY and CREATIVITY. He or she may get frustrated WAITING FOR THE GROUP. There is also a LACK OF INDIVIDUAL ACCOUNTABILITY in this pole.

In order to keep in the upper two quadrants of this polarity, the group will have to resist the pressure to over-centralize. Individuals will have to let go of being in on all the decisions in order to gain the freedom to make some on their own. There will also have to be much latitude and support for individuals or subgroups when they make mistakes.

Seeing the whole polarity and the decision continuum can help. With them, it becomes easier to see that the goal is not Participatory Management and the goal is not decentralized decision making. The goal is to manage these two polarities well by getting the best of both poles while minimizing the downsides of each pole.

Decision making needs to move UP as well as DOWN the hierarchy. Also, within the work group, the decision making needs to move IN as well as OUT. The movements DOWN and OUT were only encouraged in this section to help your organization self-correct from a past in which the emphasis was probably on the other poles.

Summary

1) Efforts at Participatory Management over the past two decades have met with mixed results. They often begin strongly but get bogged down. Because of these mixed results, there is increasing resistance to Participatory Management experiments. I suggest that Participatory Management is neither the saving solution to today's organizations nor a misguided disaster. It seems to be a needed shift in emphasis which involves at least the two key polarities: "Autocratic/Participatory" and "Centralized (Retained) Decisions/Decentralized (Delegated) Decisions."

2) Participatory Management and decentralized decision making are not automatically the same thing. Often the group becomes the new center for decisions in Participatory Management experiments. The experiment will not work very well if this happens. Groups need to delegate *out* to their membership most of the decisions at hand and be very thoughtful about it or the experiment will result in meeting paralysis.

3) Within the group, two types of resistance to pushing decisions out to subgroups and individuals are: 1) The desire of everyone to be in on all decisions, and 2) The fear of the burden of individual mistakes.

4) Decentralization is also not a solution to the management of the future. It, too, is one necessary opposite of a polarity to be managed. The other pole, centralization, must be incorporated into the picture and the process or it will not work.

5) At times, two significant yet different polarities are seen as one and the same. When this happens, separate the two and make sure each are being managed well.

Exercise

Think of a Participatory Management experiment you have been a part of or one about which you have read. What were some of the positive early outcomes? What were some of the concerns that started to emerge as time went on?

What might you do to help keep an experiment in Participatory Management from either getting bogged down in the downsides of the participatory pole or flipping back to the autocratic and getting bogged down in the downsides of that pole?

Suggestion: Discussing it as a polarity to manage helps. If you have autonomous work groups, employee involvement groups, or other types of self-regulating work groups, you might explain the polarity model to them. Have the group fill out the four quadrants with you. Then identify those who are most resistant to each pole and talk about how they can help keep the group from getting too bogged down in the pole they want to avoid. The job in polarity management is not just to protect your favorite pole but to help the group stay primarily in the upper two quadrants. Look at it as an experiment in which you learn and improve as you go along.

SECTION D
The Joys of Stress and Tranquility

The Joys of Stress and Tranquility

This polarity came up when I was working with a number of older managers who were looking at stress in their lives. Some were facing retirement in the near future. Looking at their situation through the lens of Polarity Management seemed to be helpful.

Stress is commonly thought of as negative. The literature on stress, however, makes a distinction between positive stress *(eustress)* and negative stress *(distress)*. Positive stress is that which we experience as *challenging* and *stimulating*. The challenge of white water canoeing, for example, is a wonderful source of eustress for me.

Negative stress occurs when we experience being *overwhelmed* rather than challenged. Sometimes I over-commit myself to clients and projects. What at first might have been a stimulating challenge, as I add more and more commitments, becomes distressing. I get *irritated* easily, my neck gets tight, and I feel overwhelmed and unable to concentrate. As that happens, I have moved from eustress to distress.

With that brief description, we have an idea of the content of the Stress pole of the "Stress and Tranquility" dilemma. It would look like the left half of Figure 39.

Figure 39:
Stress and Tranquility

L+		R+
Eustress Stimulating Challenging	Relaxing Replenishing Rejuvenating	
STRESS		**TRANQUILITY**
Distress Overwhelming Irritating	Boring Unstimulating Unchallenging	
L–		R–

TRANQUILITY or RELAXATION is commonly thought of as positive. Yet research on retirement suggests that there can be a downside to a life of tranquility without the benefits of eustress.

When I have been working too hard for too long and am starting to feel drained, I welcome the chance to get away from it all, relax, and get REPLENISHED. What I want and need is the upside of tranquility. It is a natural reaction to seek it out. We all know that learning to relax is a helpful response when we are "stressed out."

At the same time, constant and total relaxation LACKS THE CHALLENGE AND STIMULATION that makes life interesting. Eventually REJUVENATION becomes BORING. This is very clear on the physical level. After a physically demanding day, a good night's sleep is a great form of relaxation. However, if you stay in bed for the next week without the stimulation and challenge of physical activity, your body will grow weak and sore. And unless you have had something to occupy your mind, you probably will be bored to tears. Thus, we have an idea of the content of the Tranquility pole, which is the right half of Figure 39 (above).

As with other dilemmas, these two apparent opposites are mutually dependent. We need both stress and tranquility in our lives. We need stimulation and relaxation, challenge and rejuvenation.

At one level, this is obvious. Yet many of us live our lives as if there is only a downside to stress and only an upside to tranquility. This perception undermines both our work life and our non-work life, including retirement. When we associate work with Distress and vacations, weekends, and retirement with Relaxation, we are seeing the dilemma as shown in Figure 40.

With this perception, it is easy to see our entire work life as a crusade toward retirement. What we know about crusading is that it is important to be aware of the upside of the pole you are crusading from and the downside of the pole toward which you are crusading. Without taking these two quadrants into account, your crusade will end up in the downside of one or both poles.

Figure 40:
Crusade Toward Retirement

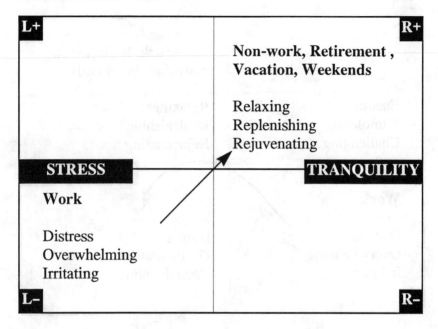

If we look at the whole polarity again, we can understand at least in part why many people find retirement so difficult after idealizing it for most of their work life.

Often people do not appreciate the eustress aspect of their work (the upside of stress - L+). They also work so long and hard at their job that their non-work life is primarily focused on relaxation (the upside of tranquility - R+). Retirement is seen as a move from Distress (L-) to Relaxation (R+).

Predictably, in Polarity Management terms, soon after retirement people find themselves in the downside of Tranquility (R-). Life lacks sufficient stimulation and challenge. The natural flow through the dilemma would have them find some eustress for their lives. This is the problem: If the only form of eustress (stimulation and chal-

Figure 41:
Retirement Syndrome

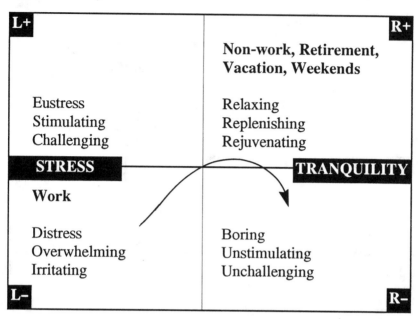

lenge) in their life was related to work, and they cannot return to work, they become trapped in the downside of tranquility (R-) and feel bored, unstimulated, and unchallenged.

The answer is to create new non-work challenges, but this seems hard for people to do without some practice before retirement. What we need to do BEFORE retirement is build tranquility into our work and eustress into our non-work lives. What that means in polarity terms is that we need to manage the "Stress and Tranquility" polarity at work, and then again in our non-work lives. This is a fundamentally different arrangement than having only one polarity with work and stress on one pole and non-work and tranquility on the other. The new arrangement would be pictured as two dilemmas side-by-side. One represents our work life and the other represents non-work life.

Figure 42:
Work and Non-work Polarities

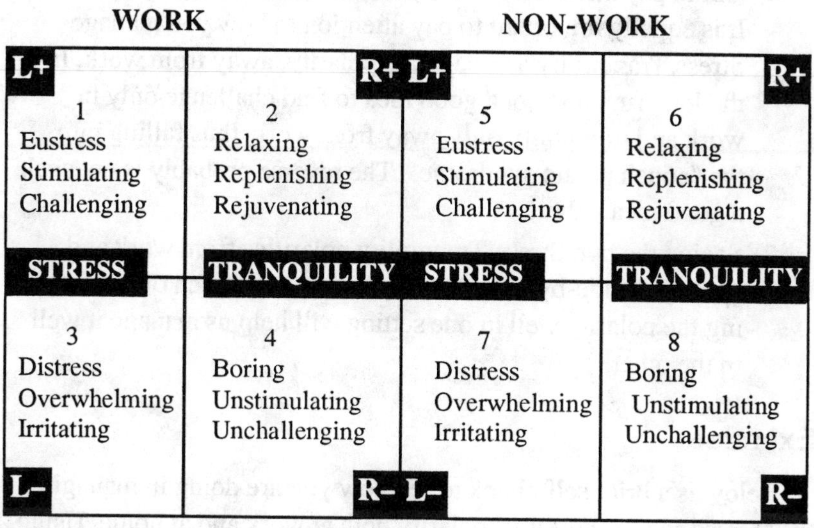

WORK		NON-WORK	
L+	**R+**	**L+**	**R+**
1	2	5	6
Eustress	Relaxing	Eustress	Relaxing
Stimulating	Replenishing	Stimulating	Replenishing
Challenging	Rejuvenating	Challenging	Rejuvenating
STRESS	**TRANQUILITY**	**STRESS**	**TRANQUILITY**
3	4	7	8
Distress	Boring	Distress	Boring
Overwhelming	Unstimulating	Overwhelming	Unstimulating
Irritating	Unchallenging	Irritating	Unchallenging
L–	**R–**	**L–**	**R–**

We need to have CHALLENGE AND REPLENISHING (1 and 2) at work as well as in our non-work (5 and 6). Many of us picture work as 3 and non-work as 6. There are six parts missing in that picture (1, 2, 4, 5, 7, and 8).

These two sets of dilemmas are interdependent. For example, if you build no relaxation into your work (2), you can easily become too tired to do anything challenging and stimulating in your non-work (5). This is assuming that you have even given yourself some non-work time!

Summary

1) We need both Eustress and Relaxation in our lives. It is important to pay attention to how you manage this polarity at work. It is equally important to pay attention to how you manage Stress/Tranquility as a separate polarity, away from work. In the long run, it is not a good idea to find challenge only in work and tranquility only away from work, thus falling into the "couch potato syndrome." The reverse probably is not such a good idea either!

2) Seeing the two Stress/Tranquility polarities from work and non-work side-by-side can help us see how much our managing the polarity well in one setting will help us manage it well in the other.

Exercise

Below is a brief self-check to see how you are doing in managing the "Stress and Tranquility" polarity both at work and at home. Using Figure 42:

A) Identify how much of 1 and 2 you have in your work life. What are some examples? Do you have enough of each?

B) Identify how much of 5 and 6 you have in your non-work life. What are some examples? Do you have enough of each?

C) What are the stimulating and challenging things in 1 and 5 that you would like to do and could do when you retire? Are there other things you would like to build into 5 so it is more available when you retire?

D) What, if anything, are you going to do about your answers to A, B and C?

SECTION E
Generic Polarities

Generic and Sister Polarities

This supplement contains three generic polarities and twenty-three sister polarities. Generic polarities are universal enough to encompass a broad spectrum of both general and individual relationships and oppositions, i.e. subgeneric divisions. It is these interrelated subgeneric divisions that I call sister polarities. They are generated by whatever generic poles are under consideration, and, as particular examples of those poles, can be said to group or "cluster" around those poles.

Part/Whole

One generic polarity I will discuss is The Part and the Whole which contains the Part. Its sister polarities include: the individual family member (part) and the family as a unit (whole that contains the part); the individual team member (part) and the team (whole); the team (part) and the department (whole); the department (part) and the company (whole); Vermont (part) and the United States (whole); the United States (part) and the United Nations (whole). From something as small as a family to something as large as the family of nations, they are all sister polarities related to each other and to the generic polarity of PART/WHOLE. The list of sister polarities to PART/WHOLE obviously could be quite large.

No matter how large the list, they all have two things in common:

1) When put in the Polarity Map, they all have the same content in their four quadrants.
2) The Polarity dynamics we have been discussing throughout the book apply to all of them. In other words, they all have Crusading and Tradition-Bearing forces at play, they all have the same normal flow through the quadrants, they all get stuck and unstuck through similar processes, and they all can be managed more or less well.

Therefore, the Polarity Management-related insights you get from managing the Individual/Team polarity at work (Chapter One) can be used to help you understand the Polarity Management-related dynamics that were involved in major global issues, such as the struggle between Lithuania (part) and the former U.S.S.R. (whole). This is one of the things that excites me about Polarity Management. It can help you and I not only become more effective leaders but also become more effective citizens, both locally and internationally. Furthermore, it can broaden our thoughts about relationships and issues, large and small, which are important to us.

Our family of nations is very large, very complicated, and can easily overwhelm us. Any perspective or set of principles that can help us transfer our understanding of a smaller, simpler system to that of a larger, more complex system, or vice versa, can reduce our frustration and give us some perspective for making a contribution. Polarity Management is just such a model and set of principles. Let us take a look at the PART/WHOLE generic polarity.

Figure 43:
Generic Part/Whole and Its "Sisters"

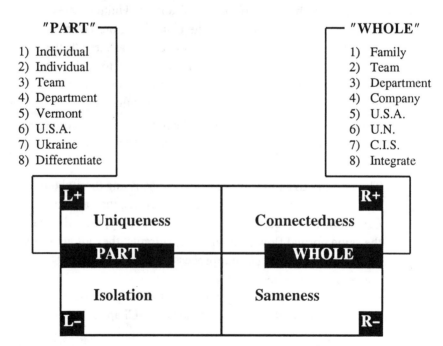

The subdivisions in the left hand column designate "parts" of a "whole," with each particular "whole" corresponding numerically in the right hand column. For example, Vermont is a "part" of the "whole" U.S.A (5/5). To say that polarities 1–8 are all sister polarities to each other and to the generic polarity of PART/ WHOLE, is to say that you could substitute any word in the left hand column for PART in the model and the corresponding word in the right hand column for WHOLE without changing the content of the four quadrants.

For example, it is important for an Individual in the Family to ex-perience UNIQUENESS (L+) within that family (1/1). It is also im-portant for a Team to experience its UNIQUENESS (L+) within a Department (3/3). No matter which combination of parallel items you use to replace PART and WHOLE in the model, the upside of focusing on the left pole will be the UNIQUENESS (L+) of the PART. Furthermore, if you emphasize the PART to the neglect of the WHOLE, the PART will fall into ISOLATION (L-). That is true whether the PART is an individual on a team (2/2) or the U.S.A. in the U.N.(6/6).

I am not saying that if you understand the dynamics of the In-dividual and Team polarity in the workplace, you automatically will know what the United States needs to do in every situation in the United Nations. What I am saying is that, in terms of the PART/ WHOLE polarity, you can have some idea about what people want and what they are afraid of as the pressures arise to move from one pole to the other. Also, the principles of managing the Individual/ Team polarity well are the same principles as managing the PART/ WHOLE aspects of the U.S.A./U.N. polarity. Seeing either pole as a "solution," for example, will lead to poor management of the polarity in both cases. If stuck in a lower quadrant, in both cases the way to get unstuck is to reverse the normal flow through the model. Under-standing the Polarity Management map and principles in relation to any sister polarity will help you get some perspective on the dynamics of any other sister polarity. It provides a context which can inform your decisions and actions in relation to the sister polarity.

For example, if a woman tells you that the United States should get out of the U.N. because it would be better for the United States, you will know she is emphasizing the PART (L) pole of the PART/WHOLE polarity. Since you have an image of this polarity model (Figure 43, above) and know the dynamics of polarities, you have an added perspective in discussing the issue with her. You know that whether the United States leaves the United Nations or not, the United States will still have to manage the PART/WHOLE polarity as long as it is a nation among nations. You know that leaving the U.N. or taking any other action which would emphasize the uniqueness of the U.S.A. is not a "solution" to this issue.

One question to ask from a Polarity Management perspective is "Will leaving the U.N. increase or decrease the ability of the United States (Part) and the world community (Whole) to manage the PART/WHOLE polarity well?" Furthermore, you know that the woman is "crusading" and that to ignore her is to reduce the likelihood of managing the polarity well, whether you support her recommendation to separate from the U.N. or not. One more thing you know is that the goal is not to defeat her efforts or to defeat those opposing her. The goal is to improve the management of this very important international polarity. I could go on about dealing with resistance and other Polarity Management principles but I do not want to repeat the book. The point is that when you see a situation in terms of a polarity to manage, all the principles involved become relevant for managing it well. Furthermore, if it is a sister polarity, the four quadrants are virtually the same, so you have quick access to what is probably motivating both the crusaders and the tradition-bearers. Finally, you have some idea about what to do to increase the likelihood that it will be managed well.

The Four Quadrants of Part/Whole

Let me return to the four quadrants of the generic polarity, PART/WHOLE. Given that these quadrants are the same for all the sister polarities, it is worth identifying their essence. I think each of us wants to experience our UNIQUENESS (L+). We like the fact that we are one of a kind. At the same time, we want to experience our CONNECTEDNESS (R+) to the rest of the world. Certainly some people prefer to be quite secluded from other people. But even they will affirm their connectedness to nature, to the plants and the other animals. It is important to be special and it is also important to belong. By contrast, it is important to avoid sameness and isolation. In more generic terms:

WITH HUMANS AND ALL HUMAN SYSTEMS, REGARD-LESS OF SIZE, THERE IS A DRIVE TOWARD EXPERIENCING OUR *UNIQUENESS* (L+) AS A DISTINCT PART WITHIN THE LARGER WHOLE.

This is a truth the opposite of which is also true: WITH HUMANS AND ALL HUMAN SYSTEMS, REGARDLESS OF SIZE, THERE IS A DRIVE TOWARD EXPERIENCING OUR *CONNECTEDNESS* (R+) AS AN INTEGRAL PART OF THE LARGER WHOLE.

These two interdependent forces are an important, underlying dynamic in all PART/WHOLE polarities. The force that is moving the system toward the PART and its UNIQUENESS is DIFFEREN-TIATION (8 in Figure 43). The force moving the system toward the WHOLE and CONNECTEDNESS is INTEGRATION (8).

The national flag of a country is a powerful symbol because it per-forms the functions of both differentiation and integration. When United States citizens are proudly waving the stars and stripes, they are differentiating themselves and their country from other countries and the citizens of those countries. It is a celebration of the unique-ness of the United States and of being a citizen of the United States. When we are focusing on our uniqueness, we are seeing ourselves as a Part in the Part/Whole polarity as in U.S.A./U.N. (6/6 in Figure 43).

At the same time, the flag-waving has an integrating effect for the United States citizens who are doing it. They are temporarily put-ting aside differences between each other, like being from Vermont, California, or other states, and highlighting the fact that we are all connected as citizens of the same country. We all belong here. When we are focusing on our connectedness, we are seeing ourselves as the Whole in the Part/Whole polarity as in Vermont/U.S.A. (5/5 in Figure 43).

The U.N. flag and Olympic flag are great symbols of another level of connectedness and integration of the community of nations. But they are not as symbolically powerful as national flags, in part because they do not perform the function of differentiation.

THERE IS MORE POWER AVAILABLE WHEN YOU CAN TAP BOTH THE DESIRE FOR UNIQUENESS AND CONNECTEDNESS THAN IF YOU JUST TAP ONE OF THEM. That is why it is important for your compensation system in an organization to recognize both individual and team performance. You are tapping both the desire for uniqueness and connectedness. Notice that the shift from one system size to another (United Nations to company) is relatively easy when working with sister polarities.

Uniqueness and Connectedness Are a Given

We *are* each unique and we *are* all connected. Everyone is special, one of a kind. So is every work team, every company and every country. The question never is whether a part is unique in a Part/Whole polarity; the question is whether the uniqueness is experienced and enjoyed by the part. Also, everyone and everything is connected. We are all part of an integrated whole. We are all one. The question never is whether the parts are connected into one whole in a Part/Whole polarity; the question is whether the connectedness or wholeness is experienced and enjoyed.

We can never lose our uniqueness, but our experience of it can diminish. When that happens, we tap the fear of losing our individuality in some undifferentiated mass (R-). The more we are expected to act the same, dress the same, and think the same, the more we will tend to fear the loss of our uniqueness. Then the drive toward differentiation of the part from the whole takes place (R- to L+).

Likewise, we can never lose our connectedness, but our experience of it can be diminished. As the experience of our connected-

214

ness is diminished, we tap the fear of losing it and becoming isolated with no sense of belonging (L-). The more we are left out or rejected, the more we will tend to fear the loss of connectedness. Then the drive toward integration of the part as an integral part of the whole takes place (L- to R+).

Labor emphasizes connectedness and talks about "solidarity." This wonderful affirmation of brotherhood and sisterhood (R+) can be pushed to the neglect of individual uniqueness. The result, in the name of unity, is excessive conformity (R-). Upper management and owners emphasize uniqueness and the reality that the higher you go up the hierarchies, the fewer there are like you. This makes you more unique within the company (L+), but it also tends to make you more isolated. Thus, the truism, "It's lonely at the top" (L-).

But what religious leaders, poets, philosophers, and mystics have been telling us for ages is that we are, each of us, precious and unique. We do not need to get to the top of an organization to experience that reality. Also, they have been telling us that we are all one. We are all interconnected and interdependent. We do not have to join any organization to experience that reality.

Such a perspective is a solid base from which to manage the Part/Whole polarity, regardless of system size. As we trust in our uniqueness as a person or our uniqueness as a company, it makes it easier for us as a part to join the whole and experience the benefits of heightening our sense of connectedness. We can do this without fear of losing our uniqueness because we know it cannot be lost. The opposite is also true. As we trust in our connectedness, it makes it easier to separate ourselves out and experience the benefits of heightening our sense of uniqueness. We can do this without the fear of losing our connectedness because we know it cannot be lost.

Thus it is possible to move back and forth primarily between the two upper quadrants of the Part/Whole polarity, experiencing our uniqueness and our connectedness, and spending very little time feeling stuck in isolation or uniformity.

Expanding the Quadrants

I have mentioned the clustering of sister polarities around the poles of a generic polarity. There is also a clustering of attributes in each of the quadrants. Below, in Figure 44, is a model of the Part/Whole generic polarity we began in Figure 43, with an ex-

Figure 44:
"Enriched" Part/Whole Polarity

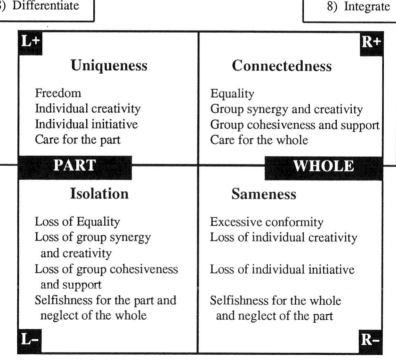

"PART"

1) Individual
2) Individual
3) Team
4) Department
5) Vermont
6) U.S.A.
7) Ukraine
8) Differentiate

"WHOLE"

1) Family
2) Team
3) Department
4) Company
5) U.S.A.
6) U.N.
7) C.I.S.
8) Integrate

L+

Uniqueness

Freedom
Individual creativity
Individual initiative
Care for the part

R+

Connectedness

Equality
Group synergy and creativity
Group cohesiveness and support
Care for the whole

PART

Isolation

Loss of Equality
Loss of group synergy
  and creativity
Loss of group cohesiveness
  and support
Selfishness for the part and
  neglect of the whole

WHOLE

Sameness

Excessive conformity
Loss of individual creativity

Loss of individual initiative

Selfishness for the whole
  and neglect of the part

L−

R−

panded list of attributes in each quadrant. The expanded lists of attributes apply to all the sister polarities. With Figure 44, you have an even richer context in which to understand the Part/Whole polarity.

You will notice that this looks similar to the Individual/Team polarity in Chapter One. That is because it is a sister polarity to PART/WHOLE. Let us swing through the four quadrants in a summary fashion. The upside of Part (L+): Associated with the desire for uniqueness is the desire for the FREEDOM to express it. Our uniqueness shows in our special CREATIVITY. Experiencing our uniqueness requires that some INITIATIVE come from us. If it comes from outside ourselves, it lacks the uniqueness that can only come from us. Finally, to value our uniqueness is to value ourselves and to CARE FOR OURSELVES. Our ability to take care of ourselves through individual initiative and creativity, as I mentioned in Chapter One, is the upside of what we call "rugged individualism." All of the above can be said about a work team, a company, or a country. If uniqueness and freedom are not being experienced by an individual, team, or nation, the drive to experience them (Crusading from R- to L+) can be very powerful. When they are experienced, the effort to keep them (Tradition-Bearing to stay in L+) can be very powerful.

The upside of Whole (R+): Associated with the desire for connectedness is the desire for EQUALITY. In religious terms, "We are all children of God." In secular terms, we say things like, "I put my pants on one leg at a time, just like everyone else." This is the area where we demand EQUAL treatment before the law. Our connectedness gives us a chance for interactive CREATIVITY and SYNERGY. GROUP COHESIVENESS gives us strength from solidarity, and we know we can count on SUPPORT from others in a time of need. We also CARE FOR THE WHOLE. That means "Not asking what your country can do for you, but what you can do for your country." If this connectedness and equality are not experienced by an individual, team, or nation, the drive to experience them (Crusading from L- to R+) can be very powerful. Also, when they are experienced, the effort to keep them (Tradition-Bearing to stay in R+) can be very powerful.

217

As you know, the downside of each pole is the opposite of the upside of the other pole. To overemphasize the Part to the neglect of the Whole leads to ISOLATION. Freedom of the Part, when pursued without concern for the whole, leads to increasing INEQUALITY and increasing isolation. The spirit of community is lost, along with its GROUP SYNERGY, COHESIVENESS AND SUPPORT. It's "every man for himself" as care for the Part becomes NEGLECT OF THE WHOLE.

There is an equal disaster in the lower right quadrant, where we find the downside of focusing on the Whole to the neglect of the Part. Dreams of equality become EXCESSIVE CONFORMITY. Group creativity and support turn into a LOSS OF INDIVIDUAL CREATIVITY AND INITIATIVE. Meanwhile, care for the whole becomes NEGLECT FOR THE PART.

When you think about the cluster of significant attributes in each of these quadrants and realize that they are present in all Part/Whole polarities, it can be a little overwhelming. Each quadrant is loaded with implications for the system in which this polarity is being managed. The benefits of managing it well are enormous on the international level and quite significant at the level of your family, work team, or company.

There is certainly a lot going on in the generic polarity of Part/Whole. But it is understandable, follows certain principles, and repeats itself in all sister polarities. In this case, the saying "If you've seen one, you've seen them all" almost fits.

Self/Other

This second generic polarity is similar to the first but warrants separate attention. Figure 45 is arranged like Figure 43, with sister polarities which can be substituted for the poles of SELF/OTHER.

The Self Pole has some obvious parallels to the Part in the Part/Whole polarity. The difference is that "Self" in this polarity is not looked at in relation to the Whole but in relation to an "OTHER" distinct entity like the Self. This distinct entity does not contain the Self

Figure 45:
Generic Self/Other and Its "Sisters"

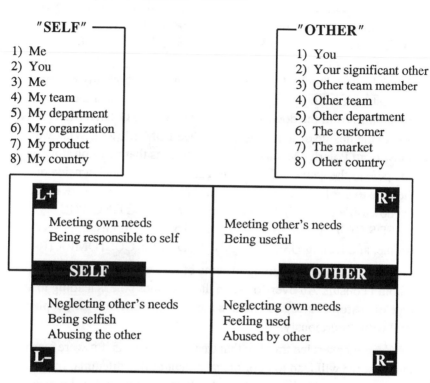

"SELF"	"OTHER"
1) Me	1) You
2) You	2) Your significant other
3) Me	3) Other team member
4) My team	4) Other team
5) My department	5) Other department
6) My organization	6) The customer
7) My product	7) The market
8) My country	8) Other country

L+	R+
Meeting own needs Being responsible to self	Meeting other's needs Being useful
SELF	**OTHER**
Neglecting other's needs Being selfish Abusing the other	Neglecting own needs Feeling used Abused by other
L–	R–

the way the Whole contains the Part. Rather than one member of the family in relation to the family, this is two individuals in the family in relation to each other.

From my perspective, I am the "Self" and You are the "Other" (1/1). From your perspective, you would be the "Self" and I would be the "Other." Let me just highlight a few aspects of this generic polarity by focusing on one of the sister polarities, My Organization/The Customer (6/6).

MEETING THE CUSTOMER'S NEEDS and BEING USEFUL to the CUSTOMER (R+) is certainly an important goal for any organization. But it is not a "solution." It is a shift in the emphasis in a polarity that organizations need to manage well.

Fill in the blank: "The _____ is always right." Try filling in any other word than "customer" and see how it feels. For example, "The boss, employee, owner, teacher, husband, wife, president, clergy, union, management, ___,____, ___,____ is always right." Do you buy it? I do not know of anyone who really believes the customer is *always* right. The slogan reflects a general crusade in our culture from the downside of focusing on the ORGANIZATION (L-) to the upside of focusing on the CUSTOMER (R+). What we know from Polarity Management principles is that concentrating on one pole to the neglect of the other leads you into the downside of the pole toward which you are crusading. In this case, we are in for the downside of the CUSTOMER pole: NEGLECTING THE NEEDS OF THE ORGANIZATION, especially its customer service people, and feeling USED and ABUSED by the CUSTOMER (R-).

This is already happening in some of the service industries with whom I consult. An over-focus on the customer pole is leading to a type of customer arrogance that is increasingly difficult for people to deal with "courteously."

Customer service training that treats this issue as if it were a problem to solve will lead to poor management of this dilemma. In our customer service training, we need to help employees see this as a dilemma to manage and then support them in developing ways to manage it. It is legitimate for them to take care of themselves *and* take care of the customer. The objective is to stay in the upper two quadrants.

It is worth mentioning that the crusade for customer service, like other crusades, stems from the downside of the opposite pole. To the degree that an organization NEGLECTED CUSTOMER NEEDS (L-) in the past, the corrective move to the other pole is both understandable and necessary. The same four quadrants are at play with any of the SELF/OTHER sister polarities listed in Figure 45 above.

To stimulate your thinking about sister polarities, here is an example list of sister polarities to the generic, Doing/Being polarity.

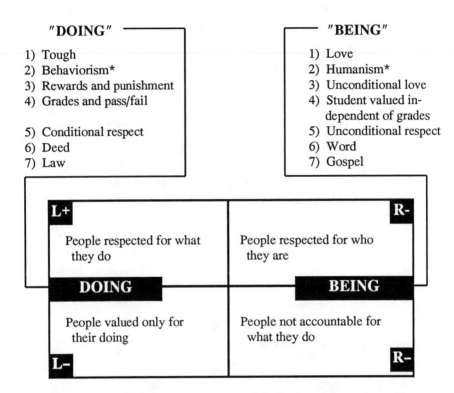

"DOING"	"BEING"
1) Tough	1) Love
2) Behaviorism*	2) Humanism*
3) Rewards and punishment	3) Unconditional love
4) Grades and pass/fail	4) Student valued independent of grades
5) Conditional respect	5) Unconditional respect
6) Deed	6) Word
7) Law	7) Gospel

L+
People respected for what they do

R-
People respected for who they are

DOING

BEING

People valued only for their doing

L-

People not accountable for what they do

R-

* Behaviorism and Humanism are not polarities in themselves. I have put them here to indicate which pole of the Doing/Being polarity each of these important disciplines tends to emphasize. To the degree each does emphasize one pole or the other, you can identify a contribution and possible limitation of each.

Special Note

In this book, I have avoided dealing with one extremely important and rich generic polarity: FEMININE/MASCULINE or YIN/YANG. The reason for not dealing with it here is that it warrants a book of its own. Pauline Lyttle and I are working on this book, as yet untitled, and are eager to share it with you as soon as possible.

SUMMARY

1) A generic polarity is so basic in nature that there are several related "sister" polarities whose upsides and downsides are virtually the same as those of the generic polarity.

2) Knowing the content of the four quadrants of all sister polarities means that you have insights into the motivations of the crusading forces and the tradition-bearing forces of all the sister polarities.

3) The sister polarities have the same dynamics between their four quadrants regardless of system size.

4) Insights you gain from learning how to manage the generic polarity or one of the sister polarities can be generalized to apply to all the other sister polarities. Thus, insights from smaller systems can help us be more effective with larger systems.

Exercise

Below are a few situations which represent sister polarities to one of the three generic polarities discussed in this chapter: Part/Whole, Self/Other, and Doing/Being. Identify the generic polarity related to each situation. Also identify what is going on in terms of the polarity model, i.e. "The system is stuck in the downside of _____."

1) Johnny has been dating Barbara for a few months. At first he loved every opportunity to help her out whenever she asked him to. He felt good about doing it and she seemed to appreciate his responsiveness and caring. This evening she called on the phone and asked if he would run to the store for her and get some typing paper for a report she was writing. For some reason, he didn't feel like going. Though he had gladly responded to similar requests earlier, the situation was starting to feel like too much somehow. What might be going on in terms of one of the generic polarities?

2) A major discussion has gone on between different plants in a multi-plant operation and the computer specialists for the system of companies. Some of the companies want a CUSTOM system made for their specific needs in order to have maximum benefit. The home office of all the companies wants an integrated COMMON system to make sure the different companies can communicate efficiently with each other. The home office "wins" and a COMMON system is put in place as the "solution" to the computer problem. Where is this system of companies likely to end up fairly soon in terms of one of the generic polarities?

3) In terms of one of the generic polarities, when Lithuania was striving for independence in its relationship with the U.S.S.R., which quadrant was it trying to move away from and which one was it trying to move toward?

Possible answers:

1) Johnny has been emphasizing the "Other" (Barbara) in the Self/Other polarity. At first he felt useful and was enjoying the upside of the "Other" pole (R+). Now, he is beginning to feel used rather than useful and is experiencing the downside of focusing on the "Other" and neglecting his own needs (R-).

2) The computer specialists are dealing with the Custom/Common polarity, which is a sister to Part/Whole. The power is with the Common (Whole) pole and they could be headed for the downside of the Common (Whole) pole.

3) Lithuania was attempting to move from the downside of Whole (R-) to the upside of Part (L+) in the Part/Whole polarity. This is understandable to the degree that they have been in a system that has, in the past, emphasized the "Whole" pole.

SECTION F
Values—The Art and Science of Polarity Management

Value-Bound Structure and Value-Free Dynamics

In this section we will look at values in relation to Polarity Management. The discussion of values will center around one of the sister polarities of the generic Part/Whole polarity described in Section E.

When working with a group on the management of a polarity, you must get their agreement of the content of the model before it can become a useful tool for them. If they do not buy into a shared polarity picture, you are dead in the water. Creating such a picture is a very subjective and artistic process. For me, this is the most enjoyable part of working with polarities. Once you have reached agreement about the content, the dynamics are predictable—like the laws of science.

Let me explain by recalling an experience. I was talking about Polarity Management with a group of national staff members of a major religious denomination. I was confronted in the middle of my presentation by one member who said, "As a denomination we have come out clearly against apartheid and are organizing against it. You seem to be saying there is an upside and a downside to everything. I don't believe it. You cannot tell me there is an upside to apartheid. So, how does your theory apply to apartheid, or doesn't it?"

His statement got my attention and everyone else's in the room. As someone opposed to apartheid myself, I was struck by the importance of his question and that I had not taken the time to look at apartheid from a Polarity perspective. This is a powerful, values-loaded issue, and since it was plopped on the table, we decided to look at it together to see if and how Polarity Management might apply. When we started out, I was not sure whether we were dealing with a problem to solve or a dilemma to manage.

The first point I made to them was that *if apartheid is part of a polarity to be managed rather than a problem to be solved, treating it as a problem to solve will reduce the likelihood of managing it well. In this case, managing such a significant polarity poorly will result in a continuation and/or escalation of the suffering.*

A second point was that *there are two places within the polarity model for things we consider wrong or evil: the lower quadrants.*

They quickly identified APARTHEID as belonging in a lower quadrant, and chose the lower left quadrant. I asked them what they wanted in their opposition to apartheid. They talked about EQUALITY (one person = one vote), RESPECT FOR OTHERS NOT IN ONE'S OWN ETHNIC GROUP, celebrating the CONNEC-TEDNESS of all people as seen in the eyes of God, the opportunity for a rich SYNERGY when diverse groups interact, and ethnic groups living together in HARMONY. This list was placed in the upper right quadrant. A list of opposite conditions (associated with apartheid) was expanded and then added to the lower left quadrant. With minimal discussion we filled out a big flip chart page which looked like:

Figure 46:
Crusading Against Apartheid

L+	Equality R+
	Respect for others
	Connectedness
	Synergy between ethnic
	groups
	Harmony
Apartheid	
Loss of equality	
Selfishness	
Isolation	
Loss of synergy	
Disharmony	
L–	R–

From a polarity perspective we can easily understand why a group seeing the situation this way would be crusading for an end to apartheid. It is also easy to see why they would have trouble understanding why anyone would resist their solution to the problem. Those resisting would easily be seen as blind or evil, or both.

Since they were crusading toward the upper right and meeting considerable resistance, Polarity Management principles would indicate that those who were resisting the crusade were hanging on to something in the upper left and extremely afraid of the lower right. If this was a dilemma to be managed and this collection of religious leaders wanted to manage it effectively, they would need to see the whole dilemma. If they could not fill out those two quadrants (L+ and R-) on their own, they would need to go to those who were resisting them and get some help.

The "neutral" axis, the line dividing the upsides from the downsides in the model, becomes important when building dilemmas that are emotionally loaded. At either end of the neutral axis there is usually a word which identifies the pole, like Individual or Team. This word should be as neutral as possible. If it is considered positive or negative, it belongs in the respective upper or lower quadrants above or below the neutral line. When you have an emotionally loaded word, like "apartheid" was for this group, in a lower quadrant, it is sometimes hard to think of a word for the upside quadrant. This is where a neutral "bridge" word can sometimes help. You can find a "bridge" word by changing the question being asked.

In this case the question changes from "What is the upside of apartheid?" to "What might be a neutral word to represent the left pole which when focused on to the neglect of the right pole leads to apartheid?" There does not have to be an upside to apartheid in order to fill in the four quadrants. To say there is an upside to apartheid would be to place apartheid on the neutral axis and claim there is an upside and a downside to it. That is a position someone might take, but that is not the position taken by this group of clergy leaders.

At this point, I had some idea about what to call the two ends of the neutral axis and what might be in the two empty quadrants. I also had an idea about how this polarity got stuck and some approaches to get it unstuck. In my efforts to find useful neutral words, I asked myself, "What are parallel words to Part/Whole, Individual/Team, Country/United Nations?" The answer was found in the two quadrants they had already filled out. We were talking about an Ethnic group (Part) among Ethnic groups (Whole). Thus I suggested Ethnicity/Multi-Ethnicity and they were willing to try it. On hindsight, it might have been more accurate to describe the two poles as Individual Racial Group (part) within a Multi-Racial Group (whole). I have chosen to leave this polarity description as it was originally created with this group. Regardless of whether we use ethnicity or race, we are still dealing with the same generic polarity of Part/Whole and the issue of one group benefiting at the expense of another. Since I am very opposed to apartheid, I found it helpful to clear my thinking by shifting to the sister polarity of Individual/ Team (Figure 14) to look for what was in the two empty quadrants of Figure 46. Once we agreed on words for the ends of the neutral axis, we had a slightly more complete picture:

Figure 47:
Identifying the "Neutral Poles"

L+		Equality R+ Respect for others Connectedness Synergy between ethnic groups Harmony
ETHNICITY		**MULTI-ETHNICITY**
Apartheid Loss of Equality Selfishness Isolation Loss of Synergy Disharmony L-		R-

The next question became: "What are the upsides of ETH-NICITY?" Notice how different this question is from asking about the upside of apartheid. Now we were talking about Polish festivals and "Black is beautiful." This is where ETHNIC UNIQUENESS is celebrated and where RESPECT FOR ONE'S OWN ETHNIC GROUP finds support. This is where ETHNIC AUTHENTICITY AND AUTONOMY receive recognition.

The final question was: "What are the downsides of focusing on MULTI-ETHNICITY to the neglect of ETHNICITY?" Here we find the LOSS OF ETHNIC UNIQUENESS AND IDENTITY as everyone gets absorbed in a pool of sameness. Respect for others becomes NEGLECT OF SELF. Pride in one's ethnicity is discouraged for fear that such differentiation will destroy the idealized harmony. With a little discussion we were able to fill in the remaining quadrants with words that reflected the values of those present.

Figure 48:
Ethnicity/Multi-Ethnicity Polarity Map

L+	R+
Freedom	Equality
Ethnic pride	Respect for others
Ethnic uniqueness	Connectedness
Ethnic initiative and	Synergy between ethnic groups
creativity	Harmony
ETHNICITY	**MULTI-ETHNICITY**
Apartheid	Loss of Freedom
Loss of Equality	Loss of Ethnic Pride
Selfishness	Neglect of Self
Isolation	Sameness
Loss of Synergy	Loss of ethnic initiative
Disharmony	and creativity
L–	R–

Our work resulted in a structure that reflected the language and values of the group. It is easy to see how the four quadrants (structure) of a polarity picture are totally dependent on the values of the group creating them. We were artists painting a picture. And, we had to work at it until the group felt it was a fair picture of reality, from *their* perspective.

Structure Is Value-Bound

Polarity Management is totally dependent on your values because it only works for you if its structure fits your values. This means that you cannot impose a polarity structure on someone else and expect it to work for them. This is the subjective, "artistic" side of Polarity Management.

Dynamics Are Value-Free

At the same time, the dynamics of Polarity Management are totally independent of your values, just like gravity. If someone supporting apartheid and someone opposed to apartheid both jump out a second story window, gravity will act on them totally independent of their values. Gravity does not discriminate. The dynamics of polarities work in the same way. Polarity dynamics do not discriminate. They work the same regardless of the values of those involved.

For example, if you locate apartheid anywhere in the polarity model, Polarity Management principles state that "over-focusing" on that pole of which apartheid is a part and neglecting the other pole will lead increasingly to the downside of the pole that contains the word "apartheid."

Furthermore, if you stay stuck in that pole long enough, you will increasingly get the downsides of both poles. This is not because that's the way it "should be" in terms of your or my value system. It is how polarities work. It is part of their dynamics. This is the objective, "scientific" side of Polarity Management.

232

We also know that if you lead a crusade from the downside of one pole to the upside of another, without being aware of the other two quadrants, you are likely to end up in one of the lower quadrants. If the tradition-bearers overpower your crusade, you will end up back in the quadrant from which you were trying to escape. If you overpower the tradition bearers, you end up in the downside of the pole toward which you were crusading.

If I had told the clergy group that apartheid was something positive and had to go in one of the two upper quadrants of the model, they would have said, "There is no sense in continuing this conversation. We do not believe in your initial premise." There is no way I could work with them on a model that did not reflect *their* values. That is what I mean when I say that the art of filling in the quadrants and two poles (structure) is based completely on your values.

But once you have filled it out, with your words and in keeping with your values, how the quadrants work in relation to each other does not depend on what is written in the quadrants. It follows the same principles (science) regardless of what is in them.

What is exciting is that Polarity Management principles have the potential to be helpful in situations where there are significant value differences to be managed. Polarity Management is dependent on people's values so it cannot be imposed. At the same time it can predict the outcome of actions regardless of the values involved.

Building Common Ground

What do you do if you have significant disagreement regarding the content of a polarity map? Use the strategy often recommended in dealing with differences: Seek common ground. The way you do that with the polarity model is as follows: Suppose you are in a group where there is a serious difference of opinion as to where "apartheid" belongs in the model. Six people see "apartheid" as a terrible injustice and do not understand how anyone could support it. For them it clearly belongs in a lower quadrant. Five people feel that "apartheid" is getting an unfair hearing outside of South Africa and that it is basi-

233

cally a good concept that is misunderstood by most people. They think it should go in an upper quadrant. Four people make up a third group, who want it to go on the neutral axis as one of the poles.

To try to get these three groups to agree on where to place the word "apartheid" in the model is worse than a waste of time. It is more likely to increase rigidity of positions and reinforce the stereotypic views they have of each other.

Instead I would divide them into three groups, based upon where they would put the word "apartheid" in the model. I would place them in separate rooms and give them 30 minutes to fill out all of the quadrants with as many items as possible, including putting "apartheid" wherever they wanted. They would put their perspectives on newsprint for presentation before the other two groups.

Each group would then show their polarity maps and report out by answering clarification questions only from other group members. Clarification questions include questions about the meaning of terms, words, phrases or questions regarding the rationale for placing a particular item in a particular quadrant.

After the three groups had a chance to clarify their models, together we would build a fourth "common ground" model made of only the content that was common to all three group models. Then we would see if the group as a whole could come up with any more content that was not on any individual group's model but that seemed to fit based on what was in the quadrants of the common ground model. Nothing would be added to the common ground model unless everyone agreed on where it should be placed in the model.

Then we would look at the polarity they had created and talk about the dynamics of all polarities and the steps to be taken for managing this polarity well. Clearly "apartheid" would not be in the "common ground" model. But that is not a problem if there is other content that they all buy into.

Notice how the process itself is one of Differentiation and Integration. The groups would be differentiated by their values and vocabulary in terms of where they wanted to place "apartheid." They would be encouraged to be different and to create their own representation of reality. The opportunity for integration would occur without asking anyone to change their picture of reality. They would all be given a chance to supplement their reality. I work with the assumption that people who feel heard are more likely to listen.

Some See It as a Problem to Solve

Some of you may still consider apartheid as a problem to solve rather than as a part of a polarity to manage. I think there are clear aspects to dealing with apartheid that are "solvable." For example, constitutional change to allow for *one person, one vote* solves the problem of voting inequality. Changing government and the abandonment of institutional practices and policies which benefit one group at the expense of another would help "solve" some of the problems with apartheid. Those are worthwhile goals, from my perspective. They represent an improvement in a system that has been stuck painfully in the downside of one pole. Those changes represent "solutions." This view makes apartheid a problem to solve and not a polarity to be managed.

What I suggest is that it may be helpful to pursue these specific solutions within the context of larger polarities. It is worth asking the questions, *"In what ways is this a problem to solve?"* and *"In what ways is it a part of a polarity to manage?"* I hope this chapter stimulates your thoughts regarding this issue.

The Merged Pole Myth

Looking at the Ethnicity/Multi-Ethnicity dilemma reminds me of a second polarity myth. I have already mentioned the One Pole Myth where people believe that if they stay on one pole they at least get the benefits of the upside of that pole even if they also experience the downside. They also believe they can avoid the downside of the other pole by staying at one pole. It is a myth you can fall into if you adopt either/or thinking.

The Merged Pole Myth can come from both/and thinking. The Merged Pole Myth is that you can merge the two upper quadrants and get the best of both poles simultaneously and avoid the two lower quadrants. I think there is some shifting back and forth between the poles of any polarity. It does not have to be dramatic, but I think it does take place. When a tightrope walker has considerable experience, there will be very little movement in the long pole used for balance. But it does move ever so slightly, shifting the emphasis from one side to the other.

When you are breathing, the managing of that dynamic process is not enhanced by an attempt to both inhale and exhale at the same time in order to get the best of both worlds! On the contrary, breathing is most effective when there is quite deep inhalation followed by quite thorough exhalation. Some polarities, like breathing, function best with a clear and intentional shift in the poles.

You can be clear AND flexible by being willing to let go of each and willing to embrace each in turn rather than simultaneously. This can be done in an instant, like seeing the goblet then the heads. It can be done in two short sentences: "I do not think we should combine these two departments." (clear) "What do you think is possible?" (flexible)

The Merged Pole Myth seems to be based in part on the natural desire to have the "best of both worlds" and to have it all at once. I think there are other aspects to the desire to merge the two upper quadrants. With merged poles, it appears you can:

1) Ignore the differences between the two poles, and

2) Avoid the need, to some degree, to let go of one in order to embrace the other.

For example, in the Ethnicity/Multi-Ethnicity dilemma, some people would just like to combine the two poles by saying things like, "I see us as one family. I do not see color. We are all just people."

These well-intentioned comments tend to lead the person to the downside of Multi-Ethnicity (R-) because they tend to undermine ethnic uniqueness. If the person could merge the poles, they would not have to deal with the ongoing choices and dynamic tensions of which pole to emphasize at any given moment.

The shifting emphasis is both necessary and healthy. It is energizing to pay attention to one's uniqueness and to one's connectedness in an ongoing play between them. This is true whether the uniqueness is as an individual or as an ethnic group. Within an ethnic group, a similar dynamic is taking place, one in which people can celebrate their uniqueness within the group and their connectedness to or membership in that group.

Those supporting the notion of merging two poles tend to think that the line between the two poles must disappear in order to establish a new sense of unity. On the contrary, with polarities, the line is part of the unity: Its interdependency is its unity.

Summary

1) The "ART" of Polarity Management is in creating the content of the Polarity map (its Structure) in a way that reflects you. The resulting "picture" is totally dependent on your values.

2) The "SCIENCE" of Polarity Management is the way the model works (its Dynamics) once you have filled it out. The dynamic relationships between the parts operate in a consistent, predictable fashion. These dynamics are totally independent of your values.

3) If you are having trouble identifying the content of a particular quadrant, it sometimes helps to find a "neutral" word to describe the pole and then look for the upside and downside of the neutral word.

4) When describing emotionally-charged polarities, certain words may be associated with strong feelings and may get in the way of someone seeing the whole picture. At those times, it may help to look for a sister polarity that is not as emotionally loaded.

5) Conflicted groups can sometimes make progress with each other by finding "common ground" in words or phrases that both sides find acceptable for each of the quadrants.

6) The MERGED POLE MYTH is the assumption that you can get rid of the line between the upside of both poles and experience them simultaneously while avoiding the downsides.

Summary and Review Exercise

This is the final exercise in the Supplement. I think it can help demonstrate that Polarity Management is both value-dependent and value free. It is also a good review of many of the principles of Polarity Management. I provide possible "lead-ins" to creating your own polarity (ART) and then describe the dynamics of whatever polarity you choose (SCIENCE).

I used this exercise to conclude a presentation on Polarity Management at an international conference a few years ago. In the room there were thirty people from six countries, speaking three languages. They helped each other create thirty individual polarity maps, and afterward I described how all their maps worked without having seen any of them.

It was great! I didn't know if the polarity they had on the paper in front of them was about their mother-in-law or two counties. It didn't matter. The polarity dynamics that I described fit for each and every polarity they had created. It demonstrated the cross-language and cross-cultural potential of Polarity Management. It also demonstrated its relevance regardless of system size.

Exercise

Create Your Own Polarity Map

Here are two suggested lead-ins to help you think of a polarity. One (I) is built from the tradition-bearing perspective. The other (II) is built from the crusading perspective. You can choose to use either lead-in or skip the lead-ins and come up with a polarity of interest to you.

  I. TRADITION-BEARING: Sometimes I'm really glad this (person, organization, country) is so (L+) _____. At those times, I want to preserve this quality by making sure this (person, organization, country) never becomes too (R-) _____.

  II. CRUSADING: Sometimes I think this (person, organization, country) is too (L-)_____. At those times, I wish this (person, organization, country) would be more (R+)_____.

Now fill in all six parts of the polarity model. I suggest you use a separate piece of paper and draw a polarity map on it like the one below. That will allow you to keep your map available alongside the book as you read through the rest of the directions.

Have you got all six parts? Do not worry if you cannot think of a name for each of the poles (L and R). What is most important is that you have something that fits for you in each of the four quadrants (L+, L-, R+, R-). If you cannot think of anything for each of the quadrants, maybe a friend or opponent can help you. If there is no help available, start over and create another polarity in which you can think of something for each of the four quadrants.

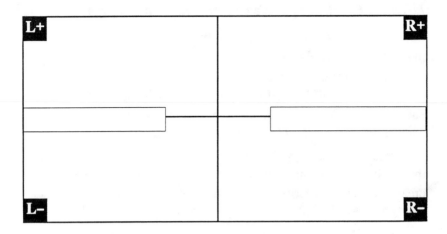

STRUCTURE BEING VALUE-DEPENDENT

Now that you have at least the four quadrants, notice how their contents are completely dependent on your values and choice of words. Others may use different words, for their values may be different. Something that you may consider positive and have placed in L+, they might consider neutral and use as a pole. Or they might consider it negative and locate it in L-. It would not work for them to force you to put what you have in L+ down into L-. You might be willing to do it in response to strong pressure, but the result would be meaningless to you because the polarity map would no longer reflect your view of reality. The imposed picture would be useless.

This demonstrates how the Polarity map cannot be effectively imposed on anyone in a way that disregards their values or their chosen words.

Is This a Problem to Solve or a Dilemma to Manage?

Now check your polarity against the two criteria which distinguish it from a problem to solve:

1) Is the difficulty ongoing?

As soon as you choose L or R, does that solve the difficulty and end the issue? Or is there an ongoing shift back and forth between L and R such that neither L nor R is a final solution?

If it is not ongoing, you probably have a problem to solve rather than a polarity to manage, in which case you need to start over and create a different polarity map in order to continue this exercise.

2) Are the two poles interdependent?

Can you just emphasize L and neglect R without having things not work well? (If you only have the four quadrants the question would be: Can you just emphasize L+ and neglect R+?)

Do L and R need each other like inhaling needs exhaling in order for either of them to be useful in the long run?

If L and R are not interdependent, you do not have a dilemma to manage and need to go back to the beginning of this exercise and create a polarity with poles that are interdependent.

DYNAMICS BEING VALUE-FREE

Now that you have a picture with at least the four quadrants filled out and it seems that there is both an ongoing shifting and interdependence between the poles, the dynamics of your picture are predictable. These dynamics will apply regardless of your values, language, or culture.

Normal Flow:

Let's start in L-. (You could start in R- if you would like. If you do, switch L+ for R+ and L- for R- in the descriptions which follow and your will see that they work equally well).

The longer and more intensely the system (person, organization, country, etc.) experiences L-, the more attractive R+ will become.

At some point there will be a shift in emphasis to R+. When that happens, the system will experience it as a good move because the system will experience some relief from L- and some of the benefits of R+. This is like inhaling when you have been exhaling for awhile.

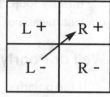

If the system stays focused on R+, especially to the neglect of L+, it will start to experience some of R-. When the system starts to experience R-, there will be a tendency to consider the previous move from L- to R+ as a mistake. This will be especially true if the system had identified L- as a "problem" and R+ as the "solution." But this is not a problem to solve, it is a polarity to manage. Therefore, R+ was neither a solution nor a mistake. It was a necessary shift in emphasis.

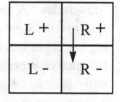

The longer and more intensely the system experiences R-, the more attractive L+ will become. Eventually there will be a shift in emphasis to L+. When that happens, the system will experience it as a good move because the system will experience some relief from R- and will experience some of the benefits of L+. This is like exhaling when you have been inhaling for a while.

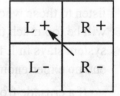

If the system stays focused on L+, especially to the neglect of R+, it will start to experience L-. When the system starts to experience L-, there will be a tendency to be self-critical for having put out so much effort to change and finding yourself back where you started some time ago.

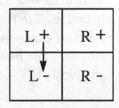

243

The familiarity of the return to L- can be very discouraging, especially if the difficulty is misperceived as a problem to be solved. When seen as a polarity to manage, the indicators of L- trigger some effort to shift the emphasis back to R+ without considering the shift to R+ as a solution and without considering the previous shift to L+ as a mistake.

Thus, we have traveled the normal flow of a polarity in an ongoing infinity loop. This is how polarities tend to flow regardless of the content in each of the four quadrants.

Well or Poorly Managed:

If the polarity you have created were well managed, the system would spend very little time in either of the lower two quadrants. It would move easily from L to R and back again, having the shift in emphasis governed by anticipation of or short experience with "downsides." A well-managed polarity would have good feedback systems that would let you know when the focus on L+ was becoming L-. There would also be a willingness to move to R+ as L- is anticipated or experienced. Likewise there would be a willingness to move back to L+ as R- is anticipated or experienced.

If the polarity were poorly managed, the system would spend unnecessary amounts of time in one or both of the two lower quadrants.

When the forces who want to emphasize L have all the power, they are less likely to listen to those who advocate R. The result will be too much time spent in L-. If the system stays in L for a very long time, it will end up experiencing both L- and R-.

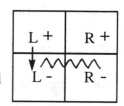

If a crusade from L- to R+ succeeds without adequate consideration for L+ and R-, the system will quickly find itself in R-. The greater the duration and intensity of the system's experience of L-, the greater the inability to see L+ and R-. And the more likely that the system will spend little time in R+ and go quickly to R-. Also, the greater the duration and intensity of the

system's experience of L-, the more it will be
willing to put up with R- because the painful
memories of L- will create great resistance to
anything that smacks of L.

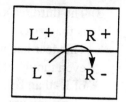

Getting Unstuck:

There are times when a system does not flow easily from one
pole to the other and back. This is usually experienced by the system
as being stuck in one of the lower quadrants. If the system is stuck in
L-, there are some reasons for the stuckness. When those reasons become understood, it becomes easier to get unstuck. Below are 3
reasons that often contribute to stuckness.

1) The first reason for stuckness is that the system is trying to
   move from a self-deprecating position. This is what happens
   when you are overly focused on L- (or R-). Those focused on
   L- without adequate vision of the other three quadrants have
   only their complaints to keep them going. Being hard on yourself or your system is not an adequate platform for change, so
   the struggle to get out of L- becomes like flailing around in
   quicksand. Paradoxically, the more you flail (or complain), the
   deeper you sink.

2) The second reason for stuckness is an extension of the first. It
   is the lack of appreciation for L+. The absence of a complete
   picture of all of L (L+ and L-) is part of what keeps the system
   from moving to R+. So to start to get the
   system unstuck, it must let go of the effort
   to follow the normal flow from L- to R+.
   Instead the system must go from L- to L+.
   The system needs to embrace all of L, including L+, in order to move to R (or R+).
   The tradition-bearing forces in the system
   are those who value L+ and are afraid of losing it. They will
   tend to oppose the move to R+. Their resistance is keeping the
   emphasis on the L pole.

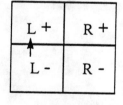

3) The third reason the system is stuck in L-
   is that part of the system is afraid of R-.
   This fear keeps the system at the L pole
   even though it may be experiencing more
   of L- than L+. The next step in the process
   of getting unstuck is to acknowledge and
   deal with R-. Without acknowledging R-,
   the tradition-bearing forces in the system
   will resist any efforts to move toward R.

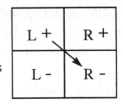

After acknowledging and somehow minimizing the possibility
of getting too much of R-, it is more likely that the system will
be able to move to R+. Thus, if a system is
stuck in the downside of one pole, it needs
to 1) explore the upsides of that pole, 2)
explore the downsides of the opposite
pole, 3) then go to the upside of the opposite pole. The process is paradoxical in
that this flow through the quadrants is the
exact opposite of the normal flow.

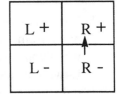

If you created a polarity to manage, the picture will reflect your
values completely. Yet how it works is completely independent of
your values.

SECTION G
Capitalism and Socialism: Neither a "Solution," Neither a "Mistake"

There are three classes of knowledge in the world: great truths, truths, and science. Great truths are those truths the opposite of which are equally true. Truths are truths the opposite of which are patently false. And science is the art of turning a great truth into a truth.
— Carl Deutch

This final section focuses on Individual and Community, another sister polarity of Part/Whole. I will use Individual and Community as a lens through which to look at capitalism and socialism. These are emotionally loaded, and many have given their lives to defend one or the other. Recognizing the power these words have for people on both sides of the issue, I do not want to be trite or simplistic about this discussion. At the same time, I do not want to avoid it. Polarity Management is especially useful in emotionally loaded situations. It is also useful in applying insights you have gained from smaller settings, like your organization or work-team, to global issues like capitalism and socialism. The reverse is also true, for insights from working with larger systems can be applied to your organization and work-team.

As you struggle with what it means to be an effective leader in an expanding, international, multicultural business setting, you are also faced with the issue of what it means to be an effective citizen of your own country and of our planet. Polarity Management can contribute to your effectiveness. This supplement will revisit many of the principles covered in the book and highlight a few new principles.

Individual and Community

I discussed polarities of Individual/Team in Chapters One and Four, and Part/Whole in Section E. Individual and Community is another sister polarity to the generic Part/Whole polarity. This means its four quadrants will be virtually the same. It also means that the dynamics between the parts will tend to be the same. So whether you are bullish on capitalism, comradish on socialism, or uncertain, your understanding of any of the sister polarities can add to the perspective as you look at capitalism and socialism.

Certainly there are other issues and other polarities to look at in the complexities of the capitalism and socialism debate. Some key polarities would include: Centralization/Decentralization, Autocratic/Democratic, and Self/Other. In this section, I am limiting the focus to one key polarity to show its potential and relevance.

With the dramatic events of 1991 in Eastern Europe and the many Republics that made up the U.S.S.R., it would be easy for those opposed to Socialism to say, "I told you so, socialism has proven itself to be a mistake." The same critics could say, "Capitalism is an obvious solution." I suggest a perceptual shift in which, contrary to the dreams of the 1917 revolution, socialism was not a "solution" in the first place and it is not a "mistake" now. It was a dramatic shift in poles from the downside of focusing on the "Part" to the upside of focusing on the "Whole." To see the move toward the other pole as a solution set it up to be called a mistake both then and 74 years later.

The other half of this perceptual shift is to see that capitalism is also neither a "solution" nor a "mistake." The capitalist tendency to emphasize the "Part" makes an important contribution to the world, and, as with all polarities, emphasizing this pole to the neglect of the other will lead to the downside of the "Part" pole. The "mistake" in this process is in overlooking the need for the ongoing management of key polarities and seeing them as problems to solve. Let us look at one of those key polarities in Figure 49. This is a familiar model which is only slightly modified from the generic Part/Whole polarity.

Both CAPITALISM and SOCIALISM value the INDIVIDUAL and the COMMUNITY. Capitalist countries and socialist countries have the upsides and the downsides of both poles. Where they differ is on which pole they put their emphasis. CAPITALISM tends to emphasize the INDIVIDUAL while SOCIALISM tends to emphasize what is best for the COMMUNITY.

Figure 49:
Individual (Capitalism)/Community (Socialism)

L+	R+
Freedom and Uniqueness	**Equality and Connectedness**
Individual creativity	Comm. synergy and creativity
Individual initiative	Comm. cohesiveness and support
"Rugged individualism"	"What is best for the most"
INDIVIDUAL (CAPITALISM)	**COMMUNITY (SOCIALISM)**
Inequality and Isolation	**Loss of Freedom and Sameness**
Loss of community and creativity	Excessive conformity
Loss of community co-hesiveness and support	Loss of individual creativity
	Loss of individual initiative
Individual selfishness and neglect of the community	Community selfishness and neglect of the individual
L-	R-

Although we in the United States value freedom and equality, our stronger emphasis is on FREEDOM. In socialist countries, there is also a value on freedom and equality, but until recently, the emphasis has been on EQUALITY: "We are all comrades."

CAPITALISM thrives on the entrepreneurial spirit of INDIVIDUAL INITIATIVE AND CREATIVITY. This orientation shows up in "rags to riches" stories highlighting the virtues of RUGGED INDIVIDUALISM and the benefits of competition. Socialism looks to

251

the collective for the SYNERGY AND CREATIVITY of group exchange. The power of COMMUNITY COHESIVENESS AND SUPPORT is highlighted along with the virtues of personal sacrifice for the common good. The focus is on "WHAT IS BEST FOR THE MOST" and the benefits of collaboration.

The two upper quadrants of the INDIVIDUAL/COMMUNITY polarity parallel the values of CAPITALISM and SOCIALISM. But there is a downside to those positive things which are valued and emphasized.

With SOCIALISM, emphasis on equality without adequate concern for freedom leads to a LOSS OF FREEDOM. Collaboration becomes EXCESSIVE CONFORMITY. INDIVIDUAL INITIATIVE AND CREATIVITY GET LOST while "WHAT IS BEST FOR THE MOST" degenerates into NEGLECT OF THE INDIVIDUAL. In other words, there is a downside to those positive things which are valued and emphasized in Socialism.

With CAPITALISM, emphasis on Freedom without adequate concern for Equality leads to gross INEQUALITY and ISOLATION of the poor from the rich. COMMUNITY SYNERGY AND CREATIVITY GET LOST along with the LOSS OF COHESIVENESS AND SUPPORT as the "haves" protect themselves from the "have nots." "Rugged individualism" degenerates into SELFISHNESS AND NEGLECT OF THE COMMUNITY. Competition becomes increasingly cut-throat and the opposition becomes more and more depersonalized. As with Socialism, there is a downside to those positive things which are valued and emphasized.

To the degree that either economic system is unable to include the opposite pole from the one it normally emphasizes, that system will not manage this polarity very well.

To the degree that socialist countries are insensitive to their tendency toward loss of freedom (R-) and are unwilling to consider the need for "rugged individualism" (L+), they will experience increasing loss of freedom and sameness (R-). Furthermore, as we know from the "one pole reality," if they rigidly and powerfully hang on to the Community pole for a long time, they will also experience more and more inequality (L-). Thus, focusing just on Equality (R+), leads to a loss of Freedom (R-), which then evolves into a loss of Equality (L-).

To the degree that capitalist countries are insensitive to their tendency toward inequality (L-) and are unwilling to consider "what is best for the most" (R+), they will experience increasing inequality and isolation (L-). Furthermore, if they rigidly and powerfully hang on to the Individual pole for a long time, they will also experience more and more loss of freedom (R-). Thus, focusing just on Freedom (L+) leads to a loss of Equality (L-) which then evolves into a loss of Freedom (R-).

Freedom and Equality are interdependent opposites; you cannot have one without the other. Crusades from within capitalist systems will emphasize equality first and freedom second because the experience of lack of freedom stems from the lack of equality. Crusades from within socialist countries will emphasize freedom first and equality second because the experience of lack of equality stems from their lack of freedom.

Trends in Business and Industry

In recent times, business and industry from socialist countries have shown an increasing interest in how to encourage the entrepreneurial spirit. This emphasis looks much like the move from (L-) to (L+) in Figure 49 (above). At the same time the emphasis in U.S. business and industry has been on collaboration and employee involvement groups. This trend is like the move from (R-) to (R+) in Figure 49.

Each is in a self-correcting shift in emphasis within its own culture.

The Crusade Toward Freedom and Uniqueness

For many reasons, there was a shift brewing in the entire Soviet culture. In terms of the Polarity Management perspective, Russia and many Eastern Block countries overemphasized and rigidly hung on to the Community pole so long that they got stuck in the downside of Community (R-) and then started experiencing the downside of Individual (L-) as well. When you look at the move from (L-) to (L+) above, are you reminded of what the upheaval has been about in many socialist countries? I am.

Sameness and excessive conformity had been experienced for so long in the Soviet Union that expressions of independence and uniqueness erupted all over the place. This drive to reaffirm uniqueness (R- to L+) shows up not only in the claims of independence made by individual republics but also in claims of uniqueness by ethnic groups within the countries.

The Crusade Toward Equality and Connectedness

There are many Central American countries we support because the leadership gives us "Freedom" to operate there; we, in turn, back the leadership's "Freedom" to take care of itself, its friends, and its families. This focus on Freedom has resulted in gross social inequality within those countries, with a concentration of more and more wealth in the hands of fewer and fewer citizens. If that inequality is not rectified, it becomes the basis for revolution. That is how we, the citizens of the United States, find ourselves backing the leadership of countries where there can be extreme inequality (L-) and loss of freedom (R-). In terms of the Polarity Management perspective, the United States and our "friendly leadership" in other countries overemphasized and rigidly hung on to the Individual pole so long that they got stuck in the downside of Individual (L-) and then started experiencing the downside of Community (R-) as well. When you look at the move from (L-) to (R+) are you reminded of what the upheaval is about in many countries whose "friendly" but isolated leadership we have supported in the past? I am.

It also corresponds to the increased inequality within the United States and between the United States and the third world. This inequality is seen not only in the concentration of wealth but also in the increasing inequality of access to health care, housing, and education. Those crusading for more equality in these areas are often criticized for promoting socialism which, the critics are quick to point out, has not had a good showing lately.

Those tradition-bearing have a point. Socialism is more clearly associated with the COMMUNITY pole. Furthermore, there is a downside to the COMMUNITY pole and an upside to the IN-DIVIDUAL pole. Their resistance is understandable and the wisdom within the resistance can contribute to the management of this polarity. At the same time, part of the reason this polarity has not been managed well in the past is due to a disproportionate amount of focus and power concentrated on the individual pole. However, this inequality, in the name of freedom, does not make Capitalism a "mistake." But neither is it a "solution." We must acknowledge the downside of our focus on the INDIVIDUAL and the upside of the focus on COMMUNITY in order to manage the polarity better.

I am not suggesting that a country has to shift its economic orientation from capitalism to socialism and back in order to manage this polarity. What is necessary is that the focus on any of the polarities in the upper left quadrant needs to be balanced by a focus on their parallel in the upper right quadrant (or the reverse). If a country emphasizes only one pole and neglects the other, it will spend unnecessary time in one or both of the lower quadrants. This will happen regardless of the values (socialist or capitalist) of the people in the country.

The real issue is not whether a country is capitalistic or socialistic or some hybrid of the two. The issue is how well the country is able to manage the polarity of Freedom and Equality, of Individual and Community. How well does a country manage it within its borders and how well does it contribute to the management of it within the community of nations?

As a planet of nations, we are not managing the Individual/Community polarity very well. One reason for the poor management is the perception that capitalism/socialism is a problem to solve. It then becomes an either/or issue with power being the deciding factor as to who "wins." But when a polarity to manage is treated like an either/ or problem to solve, no matter who wins, the larger system loses. You end up in one of the lower quadrants and the dilemma is not managed well.

As the processes of crusading and tradition-bearing go on within and between nations, those who are able to distinguish between problems to be solved and polarities to be managed, seeing the polarities holistically and managing them well, will be making a significant contribution both to their own nation and to the community of nations.

The Inability of Crusaders to See the Whole Dilemma

There are two major factors which reduce the crusader's ability to see the whole dilemma:

1) DURATION

The longer an individual or group experiences one of the lower quadrants, the more attractive becomes the upper quadrant of the opposite pole and the more difficult it is to see any upside to the present pole or any downside to the other pole.

2) INTENSITY

The more intense the negative experience in a particular lower quadrant, the more powerful is the crusade to the upside of the opposite pole. Consistent with that, the greater the intensity, the more difficult it is to see the upside of the present pole and the downside of the "ideal" place to which one wants to go. When you combine long duration with a high intensity of suffering, the ability to see all four quadrants is radically impaired.

Throughout history, there have been crusades (revolutions) launched from each of the lower quadrants of Figure 49 (above). We just looked at crusades which ended the U.S.S.R., carried out by individuals and nations who have experienced the downsides of socialism (COMMUNITY) and now long for the upsides of capitalism (INDIVIDUAL). The greater the duration and intensity of their pain in the lower right quadrant, the stronger will be their passion for the upper left. And the more difficult it will be for them to see the upsides of socialism and the downsides of capitalism.

Furthermore, Soviet citizens who have fled to the United States understandably become strong capitalism tradition-bearers. The strength of their tradition-bearing comes from the length and intensity of their prior experience. They will be the ones most sensitive to anything that smacks of socialism and try to prevent it from occurring in their new homeland. They will also put up with a considerable amount of the downsides of capitalism, if they experience them, because of their bitter memories.

Recent crusades (revolutions) in capitalist dictatorships in Central America have come from people who have experienced the downsides of capitalism and long for the upsides of socialism. Again, the greater the duration and intensity of their pain in the lower left quadrant, the stronger will be their passion for the upper right, and the more difficult it will be for them to see the upsides of capitalism and the downsides of socialism.

Furthermore, when their revolution succeeds, they understandably become strong socialist tradition-bearers. The strength of their tradition-bearing comes from the length and intensity of their prior experience. They will be the ones most sensitive to anything which smacks of capitalism and try to prevent it from occurring in their homeland. They will put up with a considerable amount of the downsides of socialism, if they experience them, because of their bitter memories of capitalism.

The long and painful experience in a lower quadrant so radically undercuts one's ability to see the whole polarity that it is extremely difficult, after arriving at the opposite pole, to keep from falling quickly into the lower quadrant of that pole.

The American Revolution was inspired by a troublesome relationship with England which seems relatively painless when compared to the painful problems experienced in other countries prior to their revolutions. This made it easier for us to be less reactive and to manage the Independent/Interdependent polarity with England much

257

better than we otherwise would have. Though we did not want a king, for example, we did create an executive branch.

Intensity and duration affect us on a smaller scale, too. Remember my experiments in Participatory Management? The same issue of intensity and duration were at play in those organizational settings. The degree to which someone has been left out of decisions about things that affect their life (intensity) and the length of time they have been left out (duration) will affect their ability to see the downside of having everyone in on all decisions. This is why it is so important that we figure out ways to minimize both the length and negativity of the time an individual, organization, or nation spends in the lower quadrants of a polarity. This is also why insensitivity to the downsides by those with most of the power is such a disaster in terms of Polarity Management.

Which brings us to the tradition-bearers and their inability to see all four quadrants.

Inability of Tradition-bearers to See the Whole Dilemma

There are two major factors which reduce the tradition-bearer's ability to see the whole dilemma.

1) INSULATION

Those who benefit most from the upside of a particular pole tend to fall out of touch with the those who benefit least and suffer most from the downside of the same pole. The greater the relative benefits a person or group has from the upside of a pole, the more they will insulate themselves from downside realities.

2) ANTICIPATED LOSS

The greater the anticipated loss from getting caught in the downside of the opposite pole, the more difficult it will be to see the upside of that opposite pole. The combination of insulation and anticipated loss make it very difficult for tradition-bearers to see the whole polarity.

There is a saying that "Those who make evolutionary change impossible make revolutionary change inevitable." This is a message to tradition-bearers. In Polarity Management terms, those who cling to one pole (and the one pole myth) will eventually get the downside of both poles and be overthrown by the increasing numbers unwilling to tolerate the downsides.

The tradition-bearers resisting change in the U.S.S.R. have some things in common with tradition-bearers in a U.S.-backed Central American dictatorship. They are tradition-bearing because they have something to lose and they believe their country has something to lose by a shift to the opposite pole. The more they have to lose, the more out of touch they are with those who feel they have little or nothing to lose. The tradition-bearers with the most to lose will tend to associate with others who have a lot to lose. Rich folks hang out with rich folks. If they can live separately, work separately, and socialize separately, they will insulate themselves from the experience of the less fortunate. If they also control the media, they can tell themselves and others that things are going fine throughout the land. All these factors and many others lead to a self-insulation from and a blindness to the downside of the present pole. This is true whether the tradition-bearer is a capitalist or a socialist. Finally, as the tradition-bearer becomes extremely afraid that a change in poles will cost him his job, his savings, his home, or his life, it becomes very difficult for him to see the upside of the opposite pole.

Thus, we can see how in either a capitalist or a socialist system, it is possible to get stuck in the downside of a pole when crusading forces and tradition-bearing forces confront each other with different views of reality. The difficulty is not that they have different views of reality. That could be a basis for learning from each other, creating a more complete picture than either has alone, and creating some ways to manage the polarity. The difficulty occurs when both the crusaders and tradition-bearers assume they have a problem to solve. They now have opposing definitions of the problem and opposing solutions. The more powerful "wins" the fight and the system ends up in the downside of one or both of the poles.

These large system examples highlight the importance of being aware of when you are dealing with a polarity to manage rather than a problem to solve. They also highlight how people can lose sight of the whole picture. It is important to understand how people can lose sight of two of the quadrants in order for you to work effectively with them on expanding their vision to all four quadrants. Once this is achieved, you can find creative ways to improve the management of the polarity.

When dealing with someone who is rigidly holding on to their incomplete picture of the quadrants, it can be helpful to consider why they are unable to see the two quadrants that would complete the picture. At that point, you might offer respect for their history, support for their "accuracy" (the reality of the two quadrants they see), and patience despite your own pressing need to have them see what you see.

Summary

1) Capitalism and socialism do not compose a polarity in itself. But the emphasis of each tends to correspond to the Individual/Community (Freedom/Equality) (Part/Whole) polarity. If you focus only on Freedom, you lose Equality first and then Freedom also. If you focus only on Equality, you lose Freedom first and then Equality also.

2) There are at least two significant factors which contribute to the inability of crusaders to see the upside of the present pole and the downside of the opposite pole: The *Duration* of their experience in the downside of the present pole and the *Intensity* of the negativity of that downside experience.

3) There are at least two significant factors that contribute to the inability of tradition-bearers to see the downside of the present pole and the upside of the opposite pole: The degree to which they have *Insulated* themselves from the realities of those benefiting least or suffering most from the present pole and the degree of *Anticipated Loss* with a shift to the other pole.

4) The inability to see the four quadrants combined with the assumption that there is a problem to solve rather than a polarity to manage results in a disastrous amount of suffering as those on both sides of the argument cling to their accuracy and miss their incompleteness.

APPENDIX
Polarities Lists

POLARITIES LISTS

PAGE

POLARITIES IN THE MAIN TEXT:

Individual and Team 7, 10, 56
Inhale and Exhale 21
Critical Analysis and Encouragement .25
Clear and Flexible 35
Planning and Action 83
Either/Or 85
My Job and My Place 94
Individual Responsibility and Organization Responsibility . .105
Well-Managed Polarity 107
Poorly Managed Polarities 108, 110, 112
Word and Deed 121

POLARITIES IN THE SUPPLEMENT:

Stability and Change 153
Conditional Respect and Unconditional Respect
            Doing and Being 168
Autocratic and Participatory 184
Centralized and Decentralized 194
Stress and Tranquility 201
Work (Stress and Tranquility)
            Non-Work (Stress and Tranquility) 205
Generic, Part and Whole 210
      Sisters:
           Individual and Family
           Individual and Team
           Team and Department
           Department and Company
           Vermont and U.S.A.
           U.S.A. and U.N.
           Lithuania and U.S.S.R.
           Differentiate and Integrate

Generic, Self and Other 219
        Sisters:
            Me and You
            You and Your Significant Other
            Me and Other Team Member
            My Team and Other Team
            My Department and Other Department
            My Organization and The Customer
            My Product and The Market
            My Country and Other Country

Generic, Doing and Being 221
        Sisters:
            Tough and Love
            Behaviorism and Humanism
            Rewards and Punishment *and* Unconditional Love
            Grades and Pass/Fail *and* Student Valued
                Independent of Grades
            Conditional Respect and Unconditional Respect
            Deed and Word
            Law and Gospel
            Differentiation and Integration

Ethnicity and Multi-Ethnicity 231

Individual and Community 251
            Capitalism and Socialism
            Freedom and Equality
            Uniqueness and Connectedness

OTHER POLARITIES:

Myers-Briggs preference polarities:
 Introversion and Extraversion
 Intuiting and Sensing
 Feeling and Thinking
 Perceiving and Judging

Rational and Emotional
Competition and Collaboration
Common Computer Systems and Custom Computer Systems
Product Engineering and Process Engineering
Style and Substance
Training for Work and Doing the Work
Means and Ends
Team Maintenance and Team Task
Right Brain and Left Brain